Better Homes and Gardens.

Gifts *from Your* Kitchen

On Cover: Gifts are (clockwise from left): *Liqueur-Flavored Wafers, Chocolate-Cream Cheese Brownies, Wine Jelly, Peanut Butter Bonbons, Holiday Divinity*, and *Cashew Brittle*. (See Index for pages.)

Above: Here is a candy jackpot with *Buttermilk Pralines*, lower left; *Holiday Divinity*, center; *Java Fudge*, upper left; and *Brown Sugar Peanut Brittle* in brandy snifter. (See Index for pages.)

BETTER HOMES AND GARDENS BOOKS

Editorial Director: Don Dooley
Managing Editor: Malcolm E. Robinson   Art Director: John Berg
Asst. Managing Editor: Lawrence D. Clayton
Asst. Art Director: Randall Yontz
Food Editor: Nancy Morton
Associate Editors: Rosemary C. Hutchinson, Sandra Granseth,
Diane Nelson, Elizabeth Strait
Assistant Editor: Flora Szatkowski
Designers: Harijs Priekulis, Faith Berven

Contents

Our seal assures you that every recipe in *Gifts from Your Kitchen* is endorsed by the Better Homes and Gardens Test Kitchen. Each recipe is carefully tested for family appeal, practicality, and deliciousness.

Make Gift-Giving Fun

Tired of racking your brain for a gift idea every time there's a special occasion? Then look through the pages of *Gifts from Your Kitchen* and discover an exciting array of presents you can make in your kitchen.

Whether it's a jar of jelly for Christmas, a box of brownies for a birthday, a cake for an anniversary, or a hearty casserole on moving day, people everywhere enjoy receiving homemade presents that say you care. Try the recipes in this book and skip the hassle of last-minute shopping.

In the first part of the book you'll chance upon a gallery of baked goods. Pick the bread, cookie, cake, or pie you need.

The second section will help you turn the fruits and vegetables you grow in your garden or discover at your local produce stand into fresh-tasting gifts. Make any of the fruit juices, soups, pickles, relishes, jellies, and jams on these pages for a gift-idea that pleases.

The pantry section is full of new foods to give. It opens with candies and also includes butters, sauces, vinegars, and seasoning mixtures. If it's easy-to-use mixes you need, they're here too, along with snacks and homemade cordials.

In the fourth part of the book, browse through the gift bazaar. Discover cookies, cakes, and breads to sell at bake sales; casseroles and salads for potluck dinners; directions for making cards and ornaments from cookie dough; and crafts from baker's clay, marzipan, and sugar ornaments.

In the final section learn all you need to know about giving gifts. Use the chart that tells how long to store foods and which ones are good mailers.

No matter what the occasion, you'll find just the present you need in *Gifts from Your Kitchen.*

Wrap an assortment of food gifts for Christmas including *Christmas Tree Bread* (see recipe, page 11), *Candy Tree, Old-Time Chewy Popcorn Balls* (see recipes, page 60), and *Rolled Sugar Cookies* (see recipe, page 17).

Taste-Tempting Gifts from the Oven

Few food gifts bring happy, appreciative smiles faster than baked goods from the oven. So for the next special occasion, treat your family or friends to one of the mouth-watering gifts in this section.

On these pages you will find an assortment of both yeast and quick breads that meet almost any gift need. For cookie fans, choose from the bar, rolled, shaped, and drop varieties. If it's a cake or pie you need, prepare one of the layer cakes, cheesecakes, fruitcakes, or fruit pies. Even steamed puddings and cupcakes are presented here. Prepare any of these recipes and you will discover how easy gift-giving can be.

Fill your kitchen with the aroma of gifts from the oven including (moving in a circle clockwise from bottom) *Julekaga, Christmas Braid, Three Kings Ring, Miniature Eggnog Coffee Cakes,* and *Festive Stollen.* (See Index for page numbers.)

Bread and Coffee Cake Classics

Festive Stollen

Enjoy this German bread shown on pages 6-7—

- ¾ cup raisins
- ½ cup chopped mixed candied fruits and peels
- ¼ cup currants
- ¼ cup rum
- 4½ to 4¾ cups all-purpose flour
- 2 packages active dry yeast
- 1 cup milk
- ½ cup butter *or* margarine
- ¼ cup sugar
- 2 eggs
- 2 tablespoons grated orange peel
- 1 tablespoon grated lemon peel
- ½ teaspoon almond extract
- ½ cup chopped almonds
- Powdered Sugar Icing

Soak raisins, mixed fruits, and currants in rum. Meanwhile, in large mixing bowl combine 1 ½ *cups* of the flour and the yeast. Heat milk, butter, sugar, and 1 teaspoon salt just till warm (115° to 120°), stirring constantly. Add to dry mixture in mixing bowl. Add eggs, peels, and almond extract. Beat at low speed of electric mixer for ½ minute, scraping bowl constantly. Beat 3 minutes at high speed. By hand, stir in fruit-rum mixture, chopped almonds, and enough of the remaining flour to make a soft dough. Turn out onto lightly floured surface; knead till smooth (8 to 10 minutes). Shape into ball. Place in greased bowl, turning once. Cover; let rise in warm place till double (1 to 1¼ hours). Punch down; divide in half. Cover; let rest 10 minutes. Roll *one half* to 12x8-inch oval. Fold long side of oval over to within ½ inch of opposite side; seal edge. Place on greased baking sheet. Repeat with remaining dough.

Cover; let rise till double (30 to 45 minutes). Bake at 375° for 15 to 20 minutes. While warm, frost with Powdered Sugar Icing. Garnish with slivered almonds if desired. Makes 2 loaves.

Powdered Sugar Icing: In a small mixing bowl thoroughly combine 1 cup sifted **powdered sugar** and enough **rum** or **milk** to make frosting of drizzling consistency.

Kugelhof

- ½ cup raisins
- ¼ cup hot water
- ¾ cup milk
- 1 13¾-ounce package hot roll mix
- 2 beaten eggs
- ¼ cup butter *or* margarine, melted
- ¼ cup sugar
- 1 teaspoon grated lemon peel
- ½ teaspoon ground mace
- ½ cup chopped walnuts

• • •

- 1 tablespoon butter *or* margarine, melted
- 3 tablespoons fine dry bread crumbs

Soak raisins in hot water. Let stand till raisins are plump. Drain; set aside. Heat milk just till warm (115° to 120°); add yeast from hot roll mix and stir till yeast is dissolved. Combine eggs, ¼ cup butter *or* margarine, sugar, lemon peel, ground mace, and yeast mixture. Add flour from hot roll mix; beat by hand till smooth. Stir in raisins and chopped walnuts. Cover; let rise in warm place till double (1½ to 2 hours).

Meanwhile brush an 8-cup fluted tube pan *or* kugelhof mold with the 1 tablespoon melted butter *or* margarine. Sprinkle bottom and sides of mold with fine dry bread crumbs. Stir down batter. Carefully spoon batter into mold; cover. Let batter rise till almost double (50 to 60 minutes). Bake at 350° for 25 to 30 minutes. Cool kugelhof in pan for 10 minutes. Remove from pan. Cool on rack. Makes 1 coffee cake.

To delight the people on your gift list, give them ❯ elegantly-shaped yeast breads such as *Kugelhof,* upper right, or one of the two shapes for *Almond Paste Twirl* (see recipe, page 10). To make an extra-special treat include a homemade jelly or jam (see recipes, pages 45 to 51) with your bread.

Three Kings Ring

This traditional Christmas favorite from Mexico is pictured on pages 6-7—

> 2½ to 2¾ cups all-purpose flour
> 1 package active dry yeast
> ⅔ cup milk
> ¼ cup butter *or* margarine
> ¼ cup granulated sugar
> ½ teaspoon salt
> 2 eggs
> ¼ teaspoon ground cinnamon
> ½ cup chopped walnuts
> ½ cup chopped mixed candied
>   fruits and peels
> 2 teaspoons grated orange
>   peel
> ½ teaspoon grated lemon peel
> Light cream *or* milk
> 1 cup sifted powdered sugar
> Candied red, green, and
>   yellow pineapple
> Walnut halves

In large mixing bowl combine *1½ cups* of the flour and the yeast. In a saucepan heat milk, butter *or* margarine, granulated sugar, and salt just till warm (115° to 120°), stirring constantly. Add milk mixture to dry mixture in mixing bowl; add eggs and cinnamon. Beat at low speed of electric mixer for ½ minute, scraping sides of bowl constantly. Beat 2 minutes at high speed. By hand, stir in chopped walnuts, the ½ cup candied fruits and peels, orange peel, lemon peel, and enough of the remaining flour to make a stiff dough. Turn out on well-floured surface. Knead till smooth and elastic (6 to 8 minutes).

Place dough in lightly greased bowl, turning once to grease surface. Cover; let rise till double (about 1½ hours). On lightly floured surface roll dough into a 26-inch rope. Carefully seal ends together to form a ring. Place on greased baking sheet. Cover; let coffee cake rise till almost double (40 to 50 minutes). Bake at 375° for 10 minutes. Cover with foil; continue baking till done, about 10 minutes more. Cool. In bowl add enough light cream to sifted powdered sugar to make of drizzling consistency. Frost cooled coffee cake. Decorate ring with "poinsettias" made out of candied pineapple pieces. Place a walnut half in the center of each poinsettia. Makes 1 coffee cake.

Almond Paste Twirl

Shape this bread, on page 9, two ways—

In mixing bowl mix 2 cups all-purpose **flour** and 1 package **active dry yeast.** Heat together 1 cup **milk,** 6 tablespoons **butter,** ⅓ cup granulated **sugar,** and ½ teaspoon **salt** just till warm (115° to 120°), stirring constantly. Add to mixture in mixing bowl; add 1 **egg.** Beat at low speed of electric mixer for ½ minute, scraping bowl. Beat 3 minutes at high speed. By hand, stir in 1 to 1¼ cups all-purpose **flour** to make a soft dough. Knead on floured surface till smooth (3 to 5 minutes). Shape into a ball. Place in greased bowl; turn once. Cover; let rise in warm place till double (1 hour). Punch down. Cover; let rest 10 minutes. Roll to 18x12-inch rectangle. Spread with Almond Filling. Starting at long end, roll as for jelly roll. Seal edge. Place seam side down diagonally (*or* shape into ring) on large greased baking sheet. Cut bread every ½ inch to within ½ inch of bottom. Pull slices alternately to the left and right. Let rise in warm place till double (45 minutes). Bake at 375° for 20 to 25 minutes. While hot sprinkle with **pearl sugar.** Makes 1.

Almond Filling: Cream ⅓ cup **sugar** and 2 tablespoons **butter.** Stir in ¼ cup **ground almonds** and ¼ teaspoon **almond extract.**

Miniature Eggnog Coffee Cakes

These tasty coffee cakes are pictured on pages 6-7—

In mixing bowl cream together ½ cup softened **butter** *or* **margarine** and 1⅓ cups granulated **sugar.** Beat in 2 **eggs.** Stir together 3 cups all-purpose **flour** and 1 tablespoon **baking powder.** Stir into creamed mixture alternately with 2 cups **eggnog.** Fold in 1 cup chopped mixed **candied fruits and peels.** Pour into greased and floured 2½-inch fluted cupcake pans *or* 2¾-inch muffin pans. Keep remaining batter refrigerated till ready to bake. Bake at 325° for 30 minutes. Remove from pans; cool on rack. Repeat with remaining batter. In bowl combine 1½ cups sifted **powdered sugar,** ¼ teaspoon ground **nutmeg,** and ¼ teaspoon ground **cinnamon.** Add enough **eggnog** to make frosting of drizzling consistency. Drizzle frosting over cooled cakes. Garnish with **candied cherry halves.** Makes 24 to 28 cakes.

Christmas Tree Bread

Make all of the shapes pictured on page 4—

> 4 cups all-purpose flour
> 1 package active dry yeast
> 1 cup milk
> ½ cup shortening
> ¼ cup granulated sugar
> 1 teaspoon salt
> 2 eggs
> 2 cups sifted powdered sugar
> 1 teaspoon vanilla
> Milk

In large mixing bowl combine *1½ cups* of the flour and the yeast. In saucepan heat 1 cup milk, shortening, granulated sugar, and salt just till warm (115° to 120°), stirring constantly. Add to dry mixture in mixing bowl; add eggs. Beat at low speed of electric mixer for ½ minute, scraping sides of bowl constantly. Beat 3 minutes at high speed. By hand, stir in enough of the remaining flour to make a moderately stiff dough. Place in greased bowl; turn once to grease surface. Cover; let rise till double (about 1 hour). Punch down; cover. Let rest 10 minutes. On floured surface roll to a 15x10-inch rectangle. Cut dough into fifteen 1-inch-wide strips.

To shape tree at left in photograph: Lay a 10-inch strip of dough on greased baking sheet for trunk. For bottom branch, piece strips of dough to form a 15-inch strip. Fold in half. Seal ends; twist. Place on trunk. Repeat using 12-, 9-, and 6-inch strips of dough.

To shape tree at center in photograph: Place a 10-inch strip of dough on greased baking sheet for trunk. Starting 1½ inches from base of trunk, place strips of dough, 9, 8, 7, 6, 5, 4, and 3 inches long on edges over trunk to form branches.

To shape tree at right in photograph: Lay a 10-inch strip of dough flat on greased baking sheet for trunk. Roll remaining pieces of dough to round slightly. Loop a 12-inch strip of dough atop trunk to form bottom branch. Repeat with 9- and 7-inch strips of dough.

Let dough rise in warm place till double (about 1¼ hours). Bake at 400° for 12 to 15 minutes. Cool. Mix powdered sugar, vanilla, and enough milk to make of spreading consistency. Drizzle over trees. Garnish with candied cherries *or* gumdrops, if desired. Makes 3.

Julekaga

Give this Scandinavian bread, pictured on pages 6-7, as a hostess gift—

> 8 to 8¼ cups all-purpose flour
> 2 packages active dry yeast
> 2 teaspoons ground cardamom
> 3 cups milk
> ½ cup butter *or* margarine
> ½ cup granulated sugar
> 2 teaspoons salt
> • • •
> ½ cup raisins
> ½ cup currants
> ½ cup chopped candied citron
> ½ cup chopped candied red cherries
> ½ cup chopped candied green cherries
> • • •
> 2 cups sifted powdered sugar
> Milk

In large mixing bowl combine *3½ cups* of the flour, the yeast, and ground cardamom. In saucepan heat together 3 cups milk, butter *or* margarine, granulated sugar, and salt just till warm (115° to 120°), stirring constantly. Add milk mixture to dry mixture in mixing bowl. Beat at low speed of electric mixer for ½ minute, scraping sides of bowl constantly. Beat 3 minutes at high speed. By hand, stir in raisins, currants, candied citron, red and green candied cherries, and enough of the remaining flour to make a moderately stiff dough.

Turn out on lightly floured surface and knead till smooth and elastic (8 to 10 minutes). Shape dough into a ball. Place dough in lightly greased bowl, turning once to grease surface. Cover; let rise in warm place till double (about 1 hour). Punch dough down. Cover. Let rest 10 minutes. Turn out on lightly floured surface. Divide dough in 3 portions. Shape each portion into a round loaf and place each in a greased 8-inch round baking pan. Cover loaves and let rise till double (about 45 minutes).

Bake at 375° for 30 minutes. Cover with foil; bake till done, about 10 minutes more. Remove loaves from pans; cool. In a small mixing bowl combine sifted powdered sugar and enough milk to make of piping consistency. Using pastry tube, pipe icing in diamond-shaped lattice atop each loaf. Makes 3 loaves.

Christmas Braid

This decorative braid is pictured on pages 6-7—

5 to 5½ cups all-purpose flour
1 package active dry yeast
2 cups milk
½ cup sugar
6 tablespoons butter *or* margarine
1 teaspoon salt
1 egg
1 cup raisins
1 cup finely chopped mixed
      candied fruits and peels
½ cup chopped Brazil nuts
1 egg yolk

In large mixing bowl combine *3 cups* of the flour and the yeast. In saucepan heat together milk, sugar, butter *or* margarine, and salt just till warm (115° to 120°), stirring constantly. Add to dry mixture in mixing bowl; add egg.

Beat at low speed of electric mixer for ½ minute, scraping sides of bowl constantly. Beat 3 minutes at high speed. Stir in raisins, candied fruits and peels, Brazil nuts, and enough of the remaining flour to make a moderately stiff dough. Turn out on floured surface. Knead till smooth and elastic (8 to 10 minutes). Place in greased bowl, turning once. Cover; let rise in warm place till double (about 1½ hours).

Divide dough into 3 portions. Then divide each portion into thirds. Roll each piece into a 15-inch rope. Place 3 ropes on a greased baking sheet. Braid. Repeat with remaining ropes, forming 3 braids. Cover and let rise in warm place till double (about 30 to 40 minutes). Combine egg yolk and 1 tablespoon water; brush some over braids. Bake at 350° for 10 minutes. Brush with more egg yolk mixture. Bake 10 minutes more. Cover with foil; continue baking 5 minutes longer. Cool. Makes 3 braids.

Few food gifts are more enjoyed and appreciated than fresh, home-baked yeast bread. The next time you need a special gift, make *Crusty White Braids,* *Sourdough-Rye Buns,* or *Whole Wheat-Molasses Bread.* To round out your gift include a chunk or wheel of your favorite cheese.

Crusty White Braids

In large bowl combine 2 cups **unbleached white flour** and 2 packages **active dry yeast.** Add 2 cups warm **water,** ¼ cup **cooking oil,** 2 tablespoons **sugar,** and 1 tablespoon **salt** to dry mixture. Beat at low speed of electric mixer for ½ minute, scraping sides of bowl. Beat 3 minutes at high speed. By hand, stir in 2 to 2½ cups **unbleached white flour** to make a moderately stiff dough. Turn out on floured surface; knead till smooth (8 to 10 minutes). Shape into a ball. Place in greased bowl; turn once. Cover; let rise till double (about 1½ hours). Punch down. Divide in half. Divide each half in thirds; shape into 6 balls. Cover; let rest 10 minutes. Roll each ball to a 16-inch rope. Line up 3 ropes, 1 inch apart, on greased baking sheet. Braid loosely, beginning in the middle. Pinch ends together; tuck under. Repeat with remaining ropes. Cover; let rise in warm place till double (40 minutes). Bake at 375°, 30 minutes. Makes 2 loaves.

Whole Wheat-Molasses Bread

In large mixing bowl combine 2¾ cups **whole wheat flour,** 1 cup **unbleached white flour,** 2 packages **active dry yeast,** and 2 tablespoons **caraway seed.** In saucepan heat 1¾ cups **water,** ½ cup **dark molasses,** ¼ cup packed **brown sugar,** 2 tablespoons **shortening,** and 1 tablespoon **salt** just till warm (115° to 120°), stirring constantly. Add to dry mixture in mixing bowl. Beat at low speed of electric mixer for ½ minute, scraping sides of bowl constantly. Beat 3 minutes at high speed. By hand, stir in ½ to 1 cup **unbleached white flour** to make a stiff dough. Turn out onto lightly floured surface; knead till smooth (5 to 8 minutes). Shape into a ball. Place dough in greased bowl, turning once to grease surface. Cover; let rise till almost double (about 1½ hours). Punch down. Divide dough in half. Cover; let rest 10 minutes. Shape into 2 slightly flattened 6-inch balls. Place on a greased baking sheet. Cover; let rise till double (about 45 minutes). Bake at 375° for 30 to 35 minutes. For chewy crust, brush each loaf with warm **water** several times during the last 10 to 15 minutes. Cool. Makes 2.

Sourdough-Rye Buns

>   Sourdough Starter
> 4½ cups whole wheat flour
> 4 cups rye flour
> ½ cup cooking oil
> ¼ cup all-purpose flour
> 1 beaten egg white
>   Coarse salt *or* caraway seed

In large bowl combine *1 cup* Sourdough Starter and 3¾ cups warm water. Stir in whole wheat flour. Beat well. Cover; let stand several hours or refrigerate overnight. Add rye flour, oil, and 1 tablespoon salt. Mix well. Dough will be slightly sticky. Knead on floured surface (5 minutes), adding all-purpose flour as necessary to make a soft dough. Place in greased bowl; turn once. Cover; let rise till double. Punch down. Divide dough in 3 portions. Cover; let rest 5 minutes. Divide each portion into 8 balls. Turn each ball in hands, folding edges under to make an even circle. Press dough flat between hands. Place on greased baking sheet, pressing each into a 3½-inch circle. Brush with egg white; sprinkle with coarse salt *or* caraway seed. Let rise till double. Bake at 375° for 25 to 30 minutes. Makes 24.

Sourdough Starter: Mix 2½ cups all-purpose **flour,** 1 package **active dry yeast,** 2½ cups warm **water,** and 1 tablespoon **honey.** Let stand, uncovered, in a glass *or* crockery jar at room temperature for 24 hours. Cover; let stand till sour, about 5 days. Stir down occasionally. (To replenish starter, add equal parts all-purpose flour and water. When starter is not in use, keep covered in refrigerator. To store several weeks, add 1 teaspoon sugar weekly.)

Gumdrop Bread

Mix 1 cup **gumdrops,** cut in small pieces and ¾ cup chopped **walnuts.** Toss; set aside. Mix 3 cups packaged **biscuit mix,** ½ cup **sugar,** and 1 teaspoon ground **cinnamon.** Add 1¼ cups **milk** and 1 beaten **egg;** stir till well combined. Fold in gumdrop mixture. Spread batter in three greased 6x3x2-inch loaf pans *or* one 9x5x3-inch loaf pan. Bake at 350° for 30 to 35 minutes for small loaves *or* 40 to 45 minutes for large loaf. Remove from pans. Cool. Wrap; store overnight. Makes 3 small or 1 large.

Raspberry-Cherry Baskets

Feature these fruit "baskets," shown on pages 86-87, as centerpieces for your next party table—

>   2 13¾-ounce packages hot roll mix
>   5 eggs
>   ¾ cup butter, softened

Using only *1 cup* warm water for both packages of roll mix, soften yeast from mixes according to package directions. In bowl beat 4 eggs well. Add yeast, roll mixes, and butter. Beat well. Cover; let rise in warm place till double (1 hour). Punch down. Turn out on floured surface. Knead a few strokes so dough is soft but not sticky. Set 2 cups aside. Spread remaining dough in 4 well-greased 9x1½-inch round baking pans. Top with Raspberry-Cherry Filling.

Divide reserved dough into 24 parts. Roll each to a 9-inch strip. Arrange 6 strips in a lattice pattern over filling in each of the pans. Beat remaining egg; brush over strips. Cover; let rise till double (30 to 45 minutes). Bake at 375° for 20 to 25 minutes. Cool 10 minutes. Remove from pans. Cool. Makes 4 "baskets."

Raspberry-Cherry Filling: Thaw one 20-ounce can frozen pitted **tart red cherries** and one 10-ounce package frozen **red raspberries.** Drain, reserving syrups. Add enough cherry syrup to raspberry syrup to make 1 cup. Blend ¾ cup **sugar,** 3 tablespoons **cornstarch,** and ¼ teaspoon **salt** in saucepan. Stir in 1 cup syrup and a few drops **red food coloring.** Cook and stir till thickened. Add fruit. Cool.

Peachy Pecan Bread

Drain one 16-ounce can **peach slices,** reserving ¼ cup syrup. Finely chop *1 cup* of the peaches; set aside. In blender container combine remaining peaches, reserved syrup, 6 tablespoons melted **butter** or **margarine, 2 eggs,** and 1 tablespoon **lemon juice.** Cover; blend just till smooth. Stir together thoroughly 2 cups all-purpose **flour,** ¾ cup **sugar,** 1 tablespoon **baking powder,** and 1 teaspoon **salt.** Add egg mixture; stir just till moistened. Fold in reserved peaches and ¾ cup chopped **pecans.** Turn into a greased 8½x4½x2½-inch loaf pan. Bake at 350° for 1 hour. Spread loaf with 2 tablespoons **peach preserves.** Cool in pan for 10 minutes. Remove; cool on rack. Makes 1.

Apple-Cinnamon Swirl Loaf

>   1 package active dry yeast
>   1 egg
>   1 package 1-layer-size white
>   cake mix
>   1 teaspoon salt
>   3½ to 3¾ cups all-purpose flour
>   2½ cups chopped peeled apple
>   ⅓ cup sugar
>   ⅓ cup chopped pecans
>   2 teaspoons ground cinnamon
>   ¼ cup butter, melted

In bowl dissolve yeast in 1¼ cups warm water (115° to 120°). Add egg, cake mix, and salt; beat till smooth. By hand, stir in enough flour to make a soft dough. Knead on floured surface till smooth. (Dough will be sticky.) Place in greased bowl; turn once. Cover; let rise till double (1¼ hours). Punch down; divide in half. Cover; let rest 10 minutes. Mix next 4 ingredients. Roll *half* of dough to 12x8-inch rectangle. Brush surface of dough with some of the butter. Sprinkle with *half* of the apple mixture. Starting at short end, roll as for jelly roll. Seal side and ends. Place in greased 8½x4½x2½-inch loaf pan. Brush top with more butter. Repeat with remaining dough, filling, and butter. Cover; let rise in warm place till double (1 hour). Bake at 375°, 30 to 35 minutes. Remove from pans; cool. Drizzle with Confectioners' Icing. Sprinkle with chopped pecans, if desired. Makes 2.

Confectioners' Icing. Blend enough light **cream** into 1 cup sifted **powdered sugar** to make of spreading consistency. Blend in ½ teaspoon **vanilla** and dash **salt.**

Cornmeal-Banana Nut Bread

In bowl stir together 1 cup **cornmeal,** 1 cup all-purpose **flour,** ½ cup **sugar,** 2 teaspoons **baking powder,** and ½ teaspoon **salt.** Mix 2 beaten **eggs,** 1 cup mashed ripe **banana,** and ⅓ *cup* **cooking oil.** Add to dry ingredients. Stir just to moisten. Fold in ½ cup chopped **walnuts.** Grease 8½x4½x2½-inch loaf pan; sprinkle additional **cornmeal** in bottom of pan. Turn flour mixture into pan. Bake at 350°, 45 to 50 minutes. Cool 10 minutes. Remove from pan; cool. Wrap; store overnight. Makes 1.

Zucchini-Ginger Bread

3 cups finely shredded unpeeled
 zucchini (about 1½ pounds)
2 cups packed brown sugar
3 eggs
½ cup cooking oil
¼ cup molasses
2 teaspoons vanilla
4 cups all-purpose flour
1 teaspoon salt
1 teaspoon baking powder
1 teaspoon baking soda
1 teaspoon ground ginger
1 cup raisins

In mixing bowl beat zucchini, sugar, and eggs
at low speed of electric mixer for 2 minutes.
Stir in oil, molasses, and vanilla. Stir together
dry ingredients. Stir into zucchini mixture.
Fold in raisins. Using five 6x3x2-inch loaf pans
or two 8½x4½x2½-inch loaf pans, fill greased
and floured pans ⅔ full. Bake at 325° 70 minutes
for small pans *or* 80 minutes for large pans. Cool
10 minutes; remove from pans. Cool. Wrap and
store overnight. Makes 5 small or 2 large loaves.

Pumpkin Coffee Loaf

⅓ cup shortening
1 cup packed brown sugar
2 eggs
1 cup canned pumpkin
¼ cup milk
1 cup all-purpose flour
1 cup whole wheat flour
2½ teaspoons baking powder
½ teaspoon salt
½ teaspoon ground ginger
½ teaspoon ground cinnamon
¼ teaspoon baking soda
¼ teaspoon ground cloves
• • •
⅓ cup chopped pumpkin seeds

Cream shortening and sugar. Add eggs, one at a
time; beat well after each. Stir in pumpkin and
milk. Stir together dry ingredients. Add to
pumpkin mixture. Beat 1 minute with electric
mixer. Stir in seeds. Bake in greased 9x5x3-inch
loaf pan at 350° 55 to 60 minutes. Cool 10
minutes. Remove from pan. Cool. Wrap; store
overnight. Makes 1.

Miniature Cherry-Date Loaves

2½ cups packaged biscuit mix
1 cup packed brown sugar
¼ cup all-purpose flour
¼ cup wheat germ
1 teaspoon ground cinnamon
3 beaten eggs
½ cup milk
¼ cup butter, melted
1⅓ cups snipped pitted dates
1 cup grated carrot
½ cup chopped maraschino
 cherries, halved
½ cup chopped walnuts

In mixing bowl stir together biscuit mix, brown
sugar, flour, wheat germ, and cinnamon.
Combine eggs, milk, and butter. Add to dry
mixture; stir just till blended. Fold in snipped
dates, grated carrot, cherries, and walnuts.
Turn into ten greased 4½x2½x1½-inch loaf
pans (*or* one 9x5x3-inch loaf pan). Bake at
350° for 20 to 25 minutes (*or* 60 minutes for
large loaf; cover with foil during the last 30
minutes of baking). Cool in pans 10 minutes.
Remove and cool on racks. Makes 10 small
loaves or 1 large loaf.

Lemon Nut Bread

¼ cup butter *or* margarine,
 softened
¾ cup sugar
2 eggs
2 teaspoons finely shredded
 lemon peel
2 cups all-purpose flour
2½ teaspoons baking powder
1 teaspoon salt
¾ cup milk
½ cup chopped walnuts

Cream together butter *or* margarine and sugar
till mixture is light and fluffy. Add eggs and
shredded lemon peel. Beat thoroughly. Stir
together flour, baking powder, and salt. Add to
creamed mixture alternately with milk, beating
well after each addition. Stir in walnuts. Pour
batter into a greased 8½x4½x2½-inch loaf pan.
Bake at 350° till done, 50 to 55 minutes. Cool
loaf in pan 10 minutes. Remove and cool on
rack. Wrap and store loaf overnight. Makes 1.

Festive Cookie Gifts

Chocolate-Cream Cheese Brownies

Easy-to-make brownies shown on page 22 —

  1 4-ounce package sweet cooking
     chocolate
  2 tablespoons butter *or* margarine
  3 eggs
1½ teaspoons vanilla
  1 cup sugar
  ½ cup all-purpose flour
  ½ teaspoon baking powder
  ½ cup chopped walnuts
  1 3-ounce package cream cheese,
     softened

Melt chocolate and butter; cool. In bowl, beat together *2* eggs and *1* teaspoon vanilla; gradually add ¾ cup sugar. Continue beating till thick and lemon-colored. Stir together flour, baking powder, and ¼ teaspoon salt; add to egg mixture. Beat well. Blend in chocolate mixture and nuts; set aside. Cream together cream cheese and ¼ *cup* sugar till fluffy. Blend in remaining egg and vanilla. Spread *half* of the chocolate mixture in a greased and floured 8x8x2-inch baking pan. Pour cheese mixture over; top with remaining chocolate mixture. Swirl layers to marble. Bake at 350°, 40 to 45 minutes. Cool. Cut into squares. Makes 16.

Maple Shortbread Bars

A variation of shortbread shown on page 58 —

1¼ cups all-purpose flour
  ¼ cup sugar
  ½ cup butter *or* margarine
  1 3½-ounce can flaked coconut
  ⅔ cup maple-flavored syrup
  ¼ teaspoon salt

Stir together flour and sugar. Cut in butter till mixture resembles fine crumbs. Press into 8x8x2-inch baking pan. Bake at 375°, 15 to 20 minutes. Meanwhile mix coconut, syrup, and salt in saucepan. Cook and stir till coconut absorbs syrup, 8 to 10 minutes. Spread over warm crumb mixture; bake 10 minutes. While warm cut into bars. Makes 2 dozen.

Spicy Pear Bars

2 cups all-purpose flour
1 cup quick-cooking rolled oats
1 cup flaked coconut
1 cup packed brown sugar
1 teaspoon baking soda
1 cup butter
4 medium pears, peeled, cored and
   chopped (2 cups)
½ cup chopped nuts
¼ cup granulated sugar
¼ teaspoon ground cinnamon
¼ teaspoon ground ginger
3 tablespoons butter

In bowl stir together flour, oats, coconut, brown sugar, soda, and ¼ teaspoon salt; cut in 1 cup butter till mixture is crumbly. Pat *half* of the mixture into a greased 15½x10½x2-inch pan. Cover with pears. Combine nuts, granulated sugar, and spices; sprinkle over fruit. Dot with 3 tablespoons butter. Pat remaining oat mixture over all. Bake at 375°, 45 to 50 minutes. While warm, cut into bars. Makes 4 dozen.

Orange-Fig Drops

  ½ cup butter, softened
  1 3-ounce package cream cheese
  ¼ cup packed brown sugar
  ⅓ cup orange marmalade
1¼ cups all-purpose flour
1½ teaspoons baking powder
  1 teaspoon ground cinnamon
  ½ cup dried figs, chopped
    Orange Frosting

Cream butter, cheese, and sugar till light. Beat in marmalade. Stir together dry ingredients and ¼ teaspoon salt; stir into creamed mixture. Fold in figs. Drop by 1½ tablespoonfuls on an ungreased cookie sheet. Bake at 350° till browned, 12 to 15 minutes. Cool. Frost with Orange Frosting. Makes 2 dozen.

Orange Frosting: Blend 1 cup sifted **powdered sugar,** ¼ cup **orange marmalade,** and 1 tablespoon softened **butter.** Beat well.

Two-Tone Cookies

Adding chocolate to half the batter for these cookies, shown on page 18, makes them two cookies in one—

- ½ cup butter *or* margarine
- ½ cup packed brown sugar
- ½ cup granulated sugar
- 1 teaspoon vanilla
- 1 egg
- ¾ cup dairy sour cream
- 1¾ cups all-purpose flour
- ½ teaspoon baking soda
- ½ teaspoon salt
- ¼ cup chopped walnuts
- 1 1-ounce square unsweetened chocolate, melted
- Walnut halves

In mixing bowl cream together butter *or* margarine, brown sugar, granulated sugar, and vanilla. Add egg; beat till fluffy. Stir in sour cream. Thoroughly stir together flour, baking soda, and salt. Gradually mix into creamed mixture; stir in chopped nuts.

Divide dough in half; stir melted chocolate into one half. Drop by rounded teaspoons 2 inches apart on an ungreased cookie sheet. Using remaining flour mixture without chocolate, drop rounded teaspoons next to each chocolate mound. (They will bake together as one.) Lightly press a walnut half onto each cookie. Bake at 375° for 12 to 15 minutes. Cool on rack. Makes 2 dozen cookies.

Suspiros

- 3 egg whites
- 1 teaspoon lemon juice
- ¼ teaspoon vanilla
- ¾ cup sugar
- ½ cup slivered almonds, toasted (2 ounces)
- 1 teaspoon grated lemon peel

Have egg whites at room temperature. Add lemon juice and vanilla. Beat to soft peaks. Gradually add sugar, beating till very stiff peaks form and sugar is dissolved. Gently fold in almonds and lemon peel. Drop from teaspoons onto a greased cookie sheet, leaving 1 inch between cookies. Bake at 275° for 35 to 40 minutes. Remove immediately onto a rack to cool. Makes 2½ to 3 dozen.

Lemon-Coconut Chews

- 1 cup butter *or* margarine
- 1 cup sugar
- 1 egg
- 2 tablespoons lemon juice
- ¼ teaspoon lemon extract
- 2½ cups all-purpose flour
- ½ teaspoon salt
- ½ teaspoon baking soda
- 1 3½-ounce can flaked coconut (1⅓ cups)
- Candied cherries, halved

Cream butter and sugar together. Add egg, lemon juice, and lemon extract; beat well. Stir together flour, salt, and soda. Add to creamed mixture; mix well. Shape into 1-inch balls; roll in coconut. Place on an ungreased cookie sheet; flatten with the bottom of a glass. Top each cookie with a candied cherry half. Bake at 375° for 10 to 12 minutes. Remove from cookie sheet immediately. Makes 7 dozen.

Rolled Sugar Cookies

Dress up these traditional favorites, pictured on page 4, by sprinkling them with colored sugar before baking or decorating them with frosting and colored candies after baking.

- ½ cup butter, softened
- 1 cup sugar
- 1 egg
- ¼ cup milk
- ½ teaspoon vanilla
- 2¼ cups all-purpose flour
- 2 teaspoons baking powder
- ½ teaspoon salt
- ½ teaspoon ground mace (optional)

Cream together butter and sugar. Add egg, milk, and vanilla; beat well. Stir together flour, baking powder, salt, and mace, if desired. Blend into creamed mixture. Divide in half. Cover; chill 1 hour. On lightly floured surface, roll each half to ⅛-inch thickness for thin cookies *or* ¼-inch thickness for thick cookies. Cut in desired shapes with cookie cutters. Place on an ungreased cookie sheet. Bake at 375°, 7 to 8 minutes for thin cookies *or* 10 to 12 minutes for thick cookies. Makes 4 to 4½ dozen thin cookies *or* 3 dozen thick cookies.

Cranberry-Pecan Tassies

    1 3-ounce package cream cheese,
        softened
    ½ cup butter, softened
    1 cup all-purpose flour
    1 egg
    ¾ cup packed brown sugar
    1 teaspoon vanilla
    ⅓ cup finely chopped fresh
        cranberries
    3 tablespoons chopped pecans

Blend cream cheese and butter. Stir in flour. If desired, chill 1 hour. Shape into twenty-four 1-inch balls; place in ungreased 1¾-inch muffin pans. Press dough evenly against bottom and sides of each. Beat together egg, sugar, vanilla, and dash salt just till smooth. Stir in cranberries and pecans. Spoon into pastry-lined muffin cups. Bake at 325°, 30 to 35 minutes. Cool in pans. Makes 2 dozen.

Diagonals

These festive cookies are pictured on pages 86-87—

Cream 1 cup **butter** *or* **margarine** and ½ cup **sugar.** Add 1 **egg;** beat well. Stir together 2½ cups all-purpose **flour** and 1 teaspoon **baking powder.** Gradually add flour mixture to creamed mixture, mixing well. Divide dough in thirds. Roll the *first third* on lightly floured surface into a 12x6-inch rectangle. Cut into three 12x2-inch strips. Place on ungreased cookie sheet. Repeat with the second third of dough. Put remaining dough in a cookie press with medium star plate. Using press make 3 lengthwise rows down center and sides of each of the strips already cut. Fill between fluted rows with **currant jelly.** Bake at 350°, 12 to 14 minutes. Cut in 1-inch diagonals. Makes 6 dozen.

◀ **Personalize your cookie gifts** with easy-to-make containers. Give *Cranberry-Pecan Tassies,* upper left, in a Red Riding Hood box made from a half-gallon milk carton. For a housewarming, have the kids decorate a shoe box as a house and put *Looped Jumbles,* upper right, in it. If you're in a hurry, wrap *Two-Tone Cookies* (see recipe, page 17) on a plate in clear plastic wrap and add a ribbon and bow.

Looped Jumbles

    ½ cup butter *or* margarine
    ½ cup sugar
    1 egg
    2 tablespoons milk
    2 cups all-purpose flour
    1 teaspoon baking powder
    ½ teaspoon ground cinnamon
    ¼ teaspoon salt
        Chocolate Glaze

Cream butter and sugar. Add egg and milk; beat till light. Stir flour, baking powder, cinnamon, and salt together. By hand, blend into creamed mixture; chill. Using a rounded teaspoon dough for each cookie, roll on a floured surface to form a 6-inch rope. Place on an ungreased cookie sheet; form a loop with ends overlapped. Bake at 375° for 8 to 10 minutes. Remove from cookie sheet. Cool on rack. Frost with Chocolate Glaze. Makes 4½ dozen cookies.

Chocolate Glaze: Melt two 1-ounce squares **unsweetened chocolate** and 2 tablespoons **butter** over low heat; stir constantly. Remove from heat; stir in 2 cups sifted **powdered sugar** and 1 teaspoon **vanilla.** Blend in enough **boiling water** (about ¼ cup) till of pouring consistency. Spoon over cookies on a rack placed over waxed paper. Reuse glaze that has dripped on waxed paper, thinning with additional boiling water, if needed.

Chocolate-Peanut Cookies

    ½ cup butter *or* margarine
    ¾ cup sugar
    1 egg
    ½ teaspoon vanilla
    1 1-ounce square unsweetened
        chocolate, melted and
        cooled
    1¼ cups all-purpose flour
    1 teaspoon baking powder
    1 cup finely chopped peanuts

Cream butter and sugar till light. Beat in egg and vanilla. Blend in chocolate. Stir together flour and baking powder; blend into creamed mixture. Chill. Shape into 1-inch balls. Roll in peanuts. Place on ungreased baking sheet about 2 inches apart; flatten with bottom of glass. Bake at 350° for 10 minutes. Makes 3 dozen.

Peanut Butter Swirls

Easy refrigerator cookies shown on page 58—

½ cup creamy peanut butter
¼ cup shortening
1 cup sugar
1 egg
2 tablespoons milk
1¼ cups all-purpose flour
½ teaspoon salt
½ teaspoon baking soda
1 6-ounce package milk chocolate
   or semisweet chocolate
   pieces, melted and cooled

Cream peanut butter, shortening, and sugar till fluffy. Beat in egg and milk. Stir together flour, salt, and soda. Stir into peanut butter mixture; blend well. Chill till firm enough to handle, 1 to 2 hours. Divide in half. Roll *half* of the dough on floured cloth to a 10x8-inch rectangle. Spread with *half* the chocolate. Starting at long side, roll as for jelly roll, using cloth to help roll. Repeat with remaining dough and chocolate. Wrap in waxed paper; chill *only* 30 minutes. (If cookie rolls are refrigerated longer, the chocolate hardens, making the rolls difficult to slice.) Slice cookies about ¼ inch thick. Place on ungreased cookie sheet. Bake at 375°, 7 to 8 minutes. Makes 4½ to 5 dozen.

Candy Window Cookies

⅓ cup butter *or* margarine
½ cup sugar
1 egg
½ teaspoon vanilla
1¼ cups all-purpose flour
½ teaspoon baking powder
¼ teaspoon salt
3 ounces hard sour candy,
   crushed

Cream together butter and sugar. Beat in egg and vanilla. Stir together flour, baking powder, and salt; stir into creamed mixture. Chill 1 hour. Roll dough ⅛ inch thick on floured surface. Cut in desired shapes. Cut out centers, leaving a ½-inch wall. Place cookies on foil-lined cookie sheet. Put ½ *teaspoon* candy in the center of each cut-out cookie. Bake at 375° till candy melts, 6 to 7 minutes. Cool and peel off foil. Makes 3½ dozen.

Mint-Cream Cheese Cookies

½ cup butter *or* margarine
1 3-ounce package cream cheese
½ cup sugar
   Few drops peppermint extract
1 cup all-purpose flour
2 teaspoons baking powder
⅛ teaspoon salt
1 cup flaked coconut
   Red *or* green maraschino
   cherries, halved

Cream together butter *or* margarine, cream cheese, sugar, and peppermint extract till light. Stir together flour, baking powder, and salt thoroughly; stir into creamed mixture just till combined. Chill 2 hours. Shape into 1-inch balls; roll each in coconut. Place on ungreased cookie sheet. Top each with half a cherry. Bake at 350° for 12 to 15 minutes. Cool on racks. Makes about 4 dozen.

Brown Sugar Spritz

Pineapple Filling
● ● ●
1 cup butter, softened
½ cup packed brown sugar
1 egg
1 teaspoon vanilla
2⅔ cups all-purpose flour
1 teaspoon baking powder

Prepare Pineapple Filling; cool. Cream butter and brown sugar. Beat in egg and vanilla. Stir together flour and baking powder; add gradually to creamed mixture, mixing till smooth. Do not chill. Place *half* of the dough in a cookie press. Using ribbon plate, press dough in ten 10-inch strips on ungreased cookie sheets. Using star plate and remaining dough, press lengthwise rows of dough on top of each strip, making a rim along both edges. Spoon Pineapple Filling between rims atop ribbon strips. Bake at 400° for 8 to 10 minutes. While hot, cut into 1¼-inch diagonals. Cool. Makes about 6½ dozen.

Pineapple Filling: In saucepan mix one 29½-ounce can **crushed pineapple,** drained, and 1 cup granulated **sugar;** bring to boiling. Simmer till very thick, 30 to 35 minutes; stir often. Divide in half. Using a few drops **food coloring,** tint filling *half* red and *half* green.

Oatmeal Party Cookies

1 cup butter, softened
1 cup sifted powdered sugar
2 tablespoons milk
2 teaspoons vanilla
2 cups all-purpose flour
1 cup quick-cooking rolled oats
1 6-ounce package semisweet
   chocolate pieces
¾ to 1 cup finely chopped walnuts

Cream together butter, sugar, milk, vanilla, and ½ teaspoon salt till light. Stir in flour and oats. Using about 2 teaspoons dough for each, shape into 1-inch balls *or* 1½-inch logs. Place on ungreased cookie sheet. Bake at 325° for 20 to 25 minutes. Cool on rack. Melt chocolate over low heat. Remove from heat; dip tops of balls *or* one end of logs in chocolate. Then dip in nuts. Let stand overnight before storing in refrigerator, if desired. Makes 4½ dozen.

Puddin' Head Gingerbread Men

You will need a gingerbread man cookie cutter for these cookies shown on page 58—

½ cup butter, softened
½ cup packed brown sugar
1 3¾- *or* 4-ounce package *regular*
   butterscotch pudding mix
1 egg
1½ cups all-purpose flour
½ teaspoon baking soda
1½ teaspoons ground ginger
½ teaspoon ground cinnamon
2 cups sifted powdered sugar
2 tablespoons frozen lemonade
   concentrate, thawed
Decorative candies

Cream butter, brown sugar, and pudding mix: add egg. Beat well. Stir together flour, soda, and spices. Stir into creamed mixture; chill. Roll dough on floured surface to ⅛-inch thickness. Cut with 4-inch gingerbread man cutter. Place on ungreased cookie sheet. Bake at 350° for 6 to 8 minutes. Remove from cookie sheet. Cool. Mix powdered sugar, lemonade concentrate, and enough water to make of spreading consistency. Frost gingerbread men *or* use pastry tube to pipe on frosting decorations. Decorate with candies. Makes 2½ dozen cookies.

Kringla

Shape these cookies, shown on pages 58 and 86-87, into a pretzel—

½ cup butter, softened
1¼ cups sugar
2 egg yolks
1 cup buttermilk
3 cups all-purpose flour
1 teaspoon baking powder
½ to 1 teaspoon ground cardamom
½ teaspoon baking soda
½ teaspoon salt

Cream butter and sugar till light. Beat in egg yolks. Blend in buttermilk. Stir together remaining ingredients. Add to creamed mixture; beat well. Divide in half. Wrap each half in waxed paper; place in freezer for 2 hours. Work with half at a time, keeping other half dough in freezer. Divide *each half* into 18 pieces. With floured hands, roll dough on floured pastry cloth into 18 ropes, 9 to 10 inches long. (Dough will be soft. Flour hands and surface often.) Bring ends of each rope together overlapping slightly to form a loop; twist ends twice. Then seal to center of opposite side forming pretzel shape. Place on lightly greased cookie sheet. Bake at 375° till browned on bottom (tops will be pale), 12 to 14 minutes. Repeat with remaining dough. Makes 3 dozen.

Apricot Refrigerator Rounds

1 cup butter *or* margarine
1½ cups packed brown sugar
1 egg
½ teaspoon almond extract
2½ cups all-purpose flour
1 teaspoon baking powder
½ teaspoon salt
1 cup finely chopped dried
   apricots
½ cup finely chopped nuts

Cream together butter and brown sugar till light. Blend in egg and almond extract. Stir together flour, baking powder, and salt; stir into creamed mixture. Stir in apricots and nuts. Shape into two rolls 1½ inches in diameter. Wrap in waxed paper. Chill well. Cut in ¼ inch slices; place on ungreased baking sheet. Bake at 350° for about 10 minutes. Makes 6½ dozen.

Jack O'Lantern Cookies

1 cup butter *or* margarine,
    softened
1½ cups granulated sugar
3 eggs
1 teaspoon vanilla
3½ cups all-purpose flour
2 teaspoons cream of tartar
1 teaspoon baking soda
½ teaspoon salt
    Light cream *or* milk
4 cups sifted powdered sugar
1 teaspoon vanilla
12 drops yellow food coloring
4 drops red food coloring
    Dash salt
    Raisins, gum drops, jelly beans,
    candy corn, and miniature
    marshmallows

In mixing bowl cream together butter *or* margarine and granulated sugar till light and fluffy. Add eggs, one at a time, beating well after each. Stir in 1 teaspoon vanilla. Stir together flour, cream of tartar, baking soda, and ½ teaspoon salt. Gradually blend into creamed mixture. Chill thoroughly, 3 to 4 hours.

On well-floured surface, roll dough ⅛ inch thick. Cut with pumpkin-shaped *or* round cookie cutter. Bake on ungreased cookie sheet at 375°, 6 to 8 minutes. Cool on rack.

Add enough cream, about 4 to 5 tablespoons, to powdered sugar to make of spreading consistency. Stir in 1 teaspoon vanilla, yellow food coloring, red food coloring, and dash salt. Spread on cookies. Decorate faces with raisins, candies, and marshmallows. Makes 5½ dozen.

◄ **Be creative when you give cookies.** For a gift that's right all year, decorate a basket with fresh flowers and heap it with *Chocolate-Cream Cheese Brownies* (see recipe, page 16). Glue your favorite fabric to a three-pound coffee can and you'll have a delightful canister for *Peanut Butter and Jelly Cookies.* Take advantage of the natural color of *Jack O'Lantern Cookies* by giving them on a plain wooden plate. For a holiday gift decorate a shoe box with green or red construction paper and gold ribbon. The window covered with clear plastic wrap lets you see the *Chocolate-Cheesecake Brownies* inside.

Peanut Butter and Jelly Cookies

Please children of all ages with the jelly filling in this sandwich cookie—

1 cup creamy peanut butter
¾ cup butter *or* margarine,
    softened
1⅓ cups sugar
3 cups all-purpose flour
2 teaspoons baking powder
½ teaspoon salt
⅓ cup milk
    ● ● ●
¼ cup grape, strawberry, *or*
    apple jelly

Cream peanut butter, butter *or* margarine, and sugar together thoroughly. Stir together flour, baking powder, and salt thoroughly. Blend into creamed mixture. Beat well. Blend in milk. Shape dough into two 2-inch rolls 7½ inches long. Wrap in clear plastic wrap. Chill for 1 hour. Slice cookies ⅛- to ¼-inch thick. Place *half of the slices,* 2 inches apart, on an ungreased cookie sheet. Spread the center of each cookie with about a ½ teaspoon jelly. Cover with remaining slices. Seal edges well with the tines of a fork. Bake at 350° for 12 to 15 minutes. Cool 1 to 2 minutes; remove from cookie sheet. Cool on rack. Makes 3 to 3½ dozen cookies.

Pizzelles

3 eggs
1 cup sugar
½ cup butter *or* margarine,
    melted and cooled
1 teaspoon vanilla
3½ cups all-purpose flour
2 *tablespoons* baking powder

Beat eggs till foamy; stir in sugar. Add cooled butter *or* margarine and vanilla. Stir flour and baking powder together thoroughly. Stir into egg mixture; mix well. Cover. Chill thoroughly. Using 2 tablespoons dough for each cookie, shape into balls. Heat a seasoned pizzelle iron on top of range over medium-high heat. Place one ball of dough at a time on iron. Squeeze lid to close; bake over gas flame *or* electric element till golden brown, about 2 minutes on each side. Turn out on rack to cool. Makes 2 dozen cookies.

Cakes to Carry

Buttermilk Spice Cake

1¾ cups all-purpose flour
¾ cup packed brown sugar
½ cup granulated sugar
1½ teaspoons ground cinnamon
1 teaspoon baking powder
1 teaspoon salt
¾ teaspoon baking soda
¼ teaspoon ground cloves
1¼ cups buttermilk
½ cup shortening
3 eggs

• • •

Vanilla Filling
Sea Foam Frosting

In mixing bowl stir together flour, sugars, cinnamon, baking powder, salt, baking soda, and cloves. Add buttermilk and shortening. Beat 2 minutes on medium speed of electric mixer. Add eggs; beat 2 minutes more. Spread batter in three greased and floured 8x1½-inch round baking pans. Bake at 350° for 20 minutes. Cool 5 minutes; remove layers from pans. Cool on racks. Fill with Vanilla Filling and frost with Sea Foam Frosting. Makes one 3-layer cake.

Vanilla Filling: In saucepan combine ⅓ cup granulated **sugar,** ¼ cup all-purpose flour, and ¼ teaspoon **salt.** Gradually add 1¼ cups **milk;** mix well. Cook and stir over medium heat till mixture thickens and bubbles; cook and stir 2 minutes longer. Very gradually stir the hot mixture into 1 beaten **egg;** return to saucepan. Cook and stir till mixture boils. Stir in 2 tablespoons **butter** *or* **margarine** and 1½ teaspoons **vanilla.** Cover surface with clear plastic wrap. Cool. (Do not stir.)

Sea Foam Frosting: In top of double boiler combine 2 **egg whites,** 1¼ cups packed **brown sugar,** ¼ cup cold **water,** 2 teaspoons **light corn syrup,** ¼ teaspoon **cream of tartar,** and dash **salt.** Beat ½ minute at low speed of electric mixer. Place over just boiling water. (Upper pan should not touch water.) Cook, beating constantly, till stiff peaks form, about 7 minutes (do not overcook). Remove from water. Beat in 1 teaspoon **vanilla.**

Chocolate Cream Cheese Cake

2 3-ounce packages cream cheese, softened
¾ cup butter, softened
1 teaspoon vanilla
6½ cups sifted powdered sugar
⅓ cup milk, at room temperature
4 1-ounce squares unsweetened chocolate, melted and cooled
3 eggs
2¼ cups all-purpose flour
1 teaspoon baking powder
1 teaspoon baking soda
1 teaspoon salt
1¼ cups milk

Cream cheese, ½ *cup* of the butter, and vanilla. Alternately beat in sugar and ⅓ cup milk. Blend in chocolate. Cover and refrigerate 2 cups mixture for frosting. Cream remaining chocolate mixture and ¼ cup butter. Add eggs; beat well. Stir together dry ingredients. Beat into creamed mixture alternately with 1¼ cups milk. Turn into two greased and floured 9x1½-inch round baking pans. Bake at 350° for 30 minutes. Cool 10 minutes; remove layers from pans. Cool on racks. Remove frosting from refrigerator 15 minutes before using. Frost cake.

Granola Ripple Cake

Make this cake, shown on page 65, with Homemade Granola Mix—

In mixing bowl combine one package 2-layer-size **white cake mix,** one 3⅝- *or* 3¾-ounce package *instant* **butterscotch pudding mix,** 1 cup **water,** and ½ cup **cooking oil.** Beat on medium speed of electric mixer till smooth, about 2 minutes. Add 4 **eggs,** one at a time, beating well after each. Pour *three-fourths* of the batter into a well-greased and floured 10-inch fluted tube pan. Sprinkle with 2 cups **Homemade Granola Mix** (see recipe, page 64). Spoon remaining batter over. Bake at 350°, 50 to 55 minutes. Cool 15 minutes; remove from pan. Cool on rack. Dust with sifted **powdered sugar.**

Citrus Cake

  ½ cup butter *or* margarine
  1¼ cups sugar
  1 egg
  ½ cup buttermilk
  1 teaspoon grated orange peel
  ⅓ cup orange juice
  3 tablespoons lemon juice
  1½ cups all-purpose flour
  1 teaspoon baking powder
  ¼ teaspoon baking soda
  ¼ teaspoon salt

Cream butter and sugar till light; add egg. Beat well. Mix in buttermilk, orange peel, and juices. Stir together dry ingredients. Stir into creamed mixture. Pour into greased 13x9x2-inch baking pan. Bake at 350°, 25 to 30 minutes. While warm frost with Citrus Frosting. Serves 15.

  Citrus Frosting: Mix 1½ cups sifted **powdered sugar**, 2 tablespoons **butter**, ½ teaspoon grated **orange peel**, 1 tablespoon **orange juice**, ¼ teaspoon grated **lemon peel**, 2 teaspoons **lemon juice**, and dash **salt**. Beat smooth.

Butter Pecan Cupcakes

  3 tablespoons butter *or* margarine
  1 cup chopped pecans
  ½ cup butter *or* margarine
  1¼ cups sugar
  2 teaspoons vanilla
  2 eggs
  2 cups all-purpose flour
  1½ teaspoons baking powder
  ⅓ cup milk
    Pecan Frosting

Dot 3 tablespoons butter over nuts in shallow baking pan. Toast in 350° oven for 15 minutes; stir often. Cream ½ cup butter and sugar till light; add vanilla. Add eggs, one at a time; beat well after each. Mix dry ingredients and ¼ teaspoon salt. Add to creamed mixture alternately with milk; beat well. Fold in ⅔ *cup* of the nuts. Reserve remaining nuts for frosting. Fill paper bake cups in 2½-inch muffin pans half full. Bake at 375°, 20 to 25 minutes. Cool. Frost with Pecan Frosting. Makes 18.

  Pecan Frosting: Mix 3 tablespoons **butter**, 3 cups sifted **powdered sugar**, ¼ cup **milk**, ¼ teaspoon **vanilla**, and reserved nuts.

Easy Lord Baltimore Cake

  1 package 2-layer-size yellow
    cake mix
  ¼ teaspoon orange extract
  1½ cups sugar
  ¼ teaspoon cream of tartar
  3 egg whites
  1 teaspoon vanilla
  ½ cup crumbled soft coconut
    macaroons (3 cookies)
  ½ cup chopped pecans
  ½ cup chopped, drained maraschino
    cherries

Prepare cake mix according to package directions *except* add orange extract. Divide batter into three greased and floured 9x1½-inch round baking pans. Bake at 350°, 14 to 16 minutes. Cool 10 minutes; remove layers from pans. Cool on racks. Mix sugar, cream of tartar, ½ cup water, and dash salt. Bring to boiling; stir till sugar dissolves. *Slowly* add sugar to egg whites; beat with electric mixer till stiff peaks form, about 7 minutes. Beat in vanilla. To *2 cups* of the frosting add remaining ingredients. Spread first layer of cake with *half* of the fruit frosting; cover with second layer. Spread with remaining fruit mixture. Top with third layer. Frost entire cake with remaining plain frosting.

Crème de Cacao Cupcakes

Mix two 1-ounce squares **unsweetened chocolate** with 3 tablespoons **water;** stir over low heat till chocolate melts. Cool. Cream ¼ cup **butter** and ½ cup granulated **sugar** till light. Add 2 **egg yolks,** one at a time, beating well after each. Blend in ½ teaspoon **vanilla** and chocolate mixture. Sift 1 cup sifted **cake flour,** ½ teaspoon **baking soda,** and ¼ teaspoon **salt.** Add to creamed mixture alternately with ¼ cup **buttermilk** and 2 tablespoons **dark crème de cacao;** beat after each addition. Beat 2 **egg whites** till stiff peaks form; fold into batter. Fill paper bake cups in 2½-inch muffin pans half full. Bake at 375°, 16 to 18 minutes. Cool. Cream ¼ cup **butter** and 2 cups sifted **powdered sugar.** Blend in ½ teaspoon **vanilla.** Add 3 to 4 tablespoons **dark crème de cacao** to make of spreading consistency. Frost cupcakes. Top with ¼ cup chopped **nuts.** Makes 14.

Butterscotch Cheesecake

1½ cups graham cracker crumbs
⅓ cup granulated sugar
6 tablespoons butter *or*
   margarine, melted

• • •

1 3¾- or 4-ounce package *regular*
   butterscotch pudding mix
½ cup granulated sugar
1½ cups milk
3 8-ounce packages cream cheese,
   softened
3 eggs
1 teaspoon vanilla

• • •

1 cup dairy sour cream
¼ cup sifted powdered sugar

In a bowl combine graham cracker crumbs, the ⅓ cup granulated sugar, and the melted butter or margarine. Carefully press into bottom and 2½ inches up sides of a 9-inch springform pan. In small saucepan combine butterscotch pudding mix and the remaining granulated sugar. Blend in milk. Cook and stir over medium heat till thickened and bubbly. Remove from heat; cover pudding surface with clear plastic wrap. Cool. In large mixing bowl beat softened cream cheese with electric mixer till fluffy; add eggs. Beat till blended. Add vanilla and the cooled pudding. Blend well.

Pour pudding mixture into crumb-lined springform pan. Bake at 375° till knife inserted just off-center comes out clean, about 50 minutes. Combine sour cream and the powdered sugar; spread atop cheesecake. Return to oven for 2 minutes more. Cool to room temperature. Remove from pan. Refrigerate. Makes 12 servings.

Directions to pack with cake. Keep refrigerated till ready to serve. Before serving garnish cheesecake with chocolate curls and banana slices dipped in lemon juice.

◄ **Beat the cooking blues** and start *Butterscotch Cheesecake* and *Easy Opera Fudge* (see recipe, page 54) with pudding mix. Dress up these recipes by adding special garnishes. For the fudge, try topping with a walnut half. Decorate the cheesecake with chocolate curls and banana slices.

Cherry Cheesecake

Mix 1¼ cups **graham cracker crumbs,** 6 tablespoons melted **butter,** and ¼ cup **sugar.** Press into bottom and 1¾ inches up sides of a 9-inch springform pan. Soften 2 packages **unflavored gelatin** in ½ cup **water.** Dissolve in double boiler over hot water. Cool. In large mixing bowl, beat 1½ cups cream-style **cottage cheese** till smooth. Add gelatin, 1½ cups **milk,** one 5½-ounce package *instant* **vanilla pudding mix,** one 3-ounce package softened **cream cheese,** and 2 tablespoons **sugar.** Beat 1 minute. Stir in ½ teaspoon grated **lemon peel,** 3 tablespoons **lemon juice,** and 1 teaspoon **vanilla.** Chill till partially set. Fold in one 16-ounce can pitted **dark sweet cherries,** drained and halved. Turn into crust. Chill 3 hours. Serves 8 to 10.

Directions to pack with cake: Keep refrigerated till ready to serve.

Pineapple Chiffon Cake

2¼ cups sifted cake flour
1½ cups granulated sugar
1 tablespoon baking powder
½ teaspoon salt
½ cup cooking oil
5 egg yolks
2 teaspoons grated lemon peel
⅔ cup unsweetened pineapple juice
8 egg whites
½ teaspoon cream of tartar
2 cups sifted powdered sugar
2 tablespoons butter, melted
2 to 3 tablespoons unsweetened
   pineapple juice

In bowl sift together flour, granulated sugar, baking powder, and salt. Make a well in center; add in order oil, egg yolks, lemon peel, and ⅔ cup pineapple juice. Beat till smooth. In large mixing bowl beat egg whites and cream of tartar till very stiff peaks form. Pour flour mixture in a thin stream over surface of egg whites; fold in gently. Bake in ungreased 10-inch tube pan at 350° 50 to 60 minutes. Invert; cool thoroughly. Remove cake from pan. Mix powdered sugar, butter, and enough of the remaining pineapple juice to make of glazing consistency. Spread over cake. Makes 1.

Double-Decker Plum Pudding

    ¾ cup shortening
    1 cup sugar
    3 eggs
    2½ cups all-purpose flour
    1 tablespoon baking powder
    1 teaspoon salt
    ½ cup milk
    ¼ cup brandy
    3 cups soft bread crumbs
        (4 slices bread)
    2 tablespoons molasses
    1 tablespoon cocoa powder
    1 tablespoon water
    ½ teaspoon ground cinnamon
    ¼ teaspoon ground nutmeg
    ¼ teaspoon ground allspice
    ⅛ teaspoon ground cloves
    1 cup snipped pitted dates
        (6 ounces)
    ½ cup chopped walnuts
        • • •
    1 cup chopped mixed candied
        fruits and peels (8 ounces)
    2 teaspoons grated orange
        peel

In large mixing bowl cream shortening and sugar; beat in eggs. Stir together flour, baking powder, and salt; stir into creamed mixture alternately with milk and brandy. Stir in soft bread crumbs. Divide batter in half (about 2¾ cups for each half).

Combine molasses, cocoa, water, and spices; blend into *half* of batter along with dates and walnuts. Turn into greased and floured 12-cup tube pan. Mix candied fruits and orange peel into remaining batter. Carefully spoon over batter in pan. Cover tightly with foil. Set tube pan in baking pan on oven rack. Pour hot water around mold to depth of 1 inch. Bake at 325° for 2 hours. Let stand in mold for 15 minutes; unmold. Makes 12 to 14 servings.

Directions to pack with pudding. Heat pudding before serving. Drizzle with some of the warm Brandy Sauce. Pass remaining sauce.

Brandy Sauce: In saucepan combine 1½ cups **sugar** and ¼ cup **cornstarch.** Stir in ¾ cup light **cream** *or* **milk.** Cook and stir till thickened and bubbly. Remove from heat. Stir in 6 tablespoons **butter** *or* **margarine,** and 3 tablespoons **brandy.**

Fruited Steamed Cranberry Pudding

    2 cups fresh cranberries
    1 cup raisins
    ½ cup chopped walnuts
    ½ cup snipped pitted dates
    1⅓ cups all-purpose flour
    ½ cup light molasses
    2 teaspoons baking soda

In bowl mix cranberries, raisins, nuts, and dates. Add flour; stir well. Mix molasses, soda, ⅓ cup boiling water, and ¼ teaspoon salt; stir into fruit mixture. Pour into greased 7-cup tube pan. Cover tightly with foil; tie with string. Place on rack in deep kettle; add boiling water to depth of 1 inch around mold. Cover; steam 1¼ hours, adding water if necessary. Cool 10 minutes; unmold. Makes 8 servings.

Directions to pack with pudding: Heat before serving. Serve with Fluffy Hard Sauce.

Fluffy Hard Sauce: Cream ½ cup softened **butter,** 2 cups sifted **powdered sugar,** and 1 teaspoon **vanilla.** Blend 1 beaten **egg yolk** into creamed mixture. Beat 1 **egg white** to stiff peaks. Carefully fold into butter mixture. Chill.

Coconut-Raisin Pound Cake

    ½ cup butter, softened
    ½ teaspoon grated lemon peel
    ¾ cup granulated sugar
    2 tablespoons lemon juice
    1 teaspoon vanilla
    3 eggs
    1½ cups all-purpose flour
    ½ teaspoon baking powder
    ½ cup milk
    ¾ cup flaked coconut
    ½ cup light raisins

Using electric mixer cream butter and peel. Slowly add granulated sugar; cream till light, about 6 minutes. Beat in lemon juice and vanilla. Add eggs, one at a time; beat 1 minute after each. Stir together flour, baking powder, and ¾ teaspoon salt; add to creamed mixture alternately with milk. Beat well after each addition. Stir in coconut and raisins. Grease *bottom only* of 8½x4½x2½-inch loaf pan; turn in batter. Bake at 325°, 1 hour 20 minutes. Cool; remove from pan. Wrap; store overnight. Dust with sifted powdered sugar, if desired.

Fast Fruitcake

>   1 package 2-layer-size spice
>   cake mix
>   1 3⅝- or 3¾-ounce package
>   *instant* lemon pudding mix
>   ⅔ cup apricot nectar
>   ½ cup cooking oil
>   ¼ cup apricot brandy
>   4 eggs
>   1 cup raisins
>   1 cup sliced candied pineapple
>   1 cup chopped walnuts

In mixing bowl combine cake and pudding mix, apricot nectar, cooking oil, and brandy. Beat on medium speed of electric mixer till smooth, about 2 minutes. Add eggs, one at a time, beating well after each. Fold in fruits and nuts. Turn into well-greased and floured 10-inch tube pan. Bake at 350° till cake tests done, 50 to 55 minutes. Cool in pan 15 minutes. Remove from pan; cool on rack. Wrap; store in refrigerator 24 hours. Give immediately. (Do not store for long periods of time.) Makes 1.

Stained Glass Fruitcakes

Colorful fruitcakes as pictured on pages 86-87—

>   4 cups pecan halves
>   3½ cups walnut halves
>   3 cups assorted colors of candied
>   pineapple, cut up
>   2¾ cups light raisins
>   1 16-ounce package whole pitted
>   dates
>   1½ cups red candied cherries
>   1½ cups green candied cherries
>   2 14-ounce cans *sweetened
>   condensed* milk

In large bowl combine nuts, fruits, and condensed milk; mix well. Wash and dry four 16-ounce cans. Line six 4½x2½x1½-inch loaf pans with foil. Grease cans and foil-lined loaf pans. Press fruit mixture into cans and pans.* Bake at 275°, 45 minutes. Cool; remove from containers. (For cans, loosen sides; remove bottom. Push cake through.) Wrap in foil *or* clear plastic wrap. Store in refrigerator for several weeks to a year. Makes 10 cakes.
  *Note: If desired, bake some of the batter in greased foil bonbon cups at 275°, 25 minutes.

Holiday Chip Cake

>   2 cups chopped mixed candied
>   fruits and peels
>   2 cups raisins
>   1½ cups chopped pecans
>   1 cup semisweet chocolate
>   pieces
>   • • •
>   ¼ cup butter *or* margarine,
>   softened
>   1 cup sugar
>   3 eggs
>   ¼ cup applesauce
>   ¼ cup water
>   1½ cups all-purpose flour
>   ¼ teaspoon baking soda
>   ¼ teaspoon ground allspice
>   ¼ teaspoon ground cinnamon
>   ¼ teaspoon instant coffee
>   granules

Lightly oil a 7-cup ring mold. Line with heavy brown paper; oil again. Mix fruits and peels, raisins, pecans, and chocolate pieces. Cream butter and sugar till fluffy. Add eggs, one at a time, beating well after each. Stir in applesauce and water. Stir together flour, soda, spices, and coffee. Stir into creamed mixture. Fold in fruit mixture. Turn into ring mold. Bake at 275°, about 2¾ hours. Cool; remove from pan. Wrap and store in cool place. Makes 1.

Brazil Nut-Date Cake

In large mixing bowl combine one 16-ounce package snipped **pitted dates**, 1½ cups **whole Brazil nuts**, 1½ cups drained **maraschino cherries**, and 1 cup **pecan halves**. Stir ¾ cup all-purpose **flour**, ¾ cup **sugar**, ½ teaspoon **baking powder**, and ½ teaspoon **salt** together thoroughly. Beat 3 **eggs** and 1 teaspoon **vanilla** till foamy. Stir in flour mixture. Pour egg mixture over nut mixture, stirring to mix well. Turn into greased, paper-lined 9x5x3-inch loaf pan. Bake at 300° till cake tests done, for 1 hour 30 minutes to 1 hour 40 minutes. Cool in pan 10 minutes. Remove from pan. Cool thoroughly. Wrap in **wine** or **brandy**-moistened cheesecloth. Overwrap in foil. Store several days in a cool place. Remoisten cheesecloth as necessary. Makes 1 cake.

Pies that Travel

Plain Pastry

Makes one 9-inch 2-crust or lattice-top pie or two 9-inch pie shells—

- 2 cups all-purpose flour
- 1 teaspoon salt
- ⅔ cup shortening
- 6 to 7 tablespoons cold water

Stir together flour and salt. Cut in shortening till the size of small peas. Sprinkle water over, 1 tablespoon at a time. Toss after each addition. Form into two balls; flatten on floured surface. Roll into two circles ⅛ inch thick.

For 2-crust pie: Line 9-inch pie plate with *half* the pastry. Trim crust even with rim of plate. Add filling. Lift remaining pastry by rolling over rolling pin. Then unroll over filled pie. Trim ½ inch beyond edge. Tuck top crust under lower crust. Flute edge, cut slits for escape of steam.

For lattice-top pie: Line 9-inch pie plate with *half* the pastry. Trim crust ½ inch beyond edge of plate. Add filling. Cut remaining dough in strips ½ to ¾ inch wide. Lay strips on filled pie at 1-inch intervals. Fold back alternate strips to center. Starting at center lay one strip crosswise. Return folded strips to original position. Repeat, turning back alternate strips to complete lattice. Trim lattice even with rim of plate. Fold lower crust over strips. Seal; flute edge.

For pie shells: Line two 9-inch pie plates with pastry. Trim pastry ½ to 1 inch beyond rim of plates. Fold under; flute edge. For baked shells, prick bottom and sides well; bake at 450°, 10 to 12 minutes. (If filling and crust are baked together, do not prick.)

Cranberry-Pecan Pie

In mixing bowl, mix 3 beaten **eggs**, 1 cup **dark corn syrup**, ⅔ cup **sugar**, ¼ cup melted **butter,** *or* **margarine,** and dash **salt.** Sprinkle 1 cup chopped fresh **cranberries** evenly into one 9-inch **unbaked pastry shell.** Pour syrup mixture over berries. Top with 1 cup **pecans.** Bake at 325° till knife inserted off-center comes out clean, 60 to 65 minutes. Cool.

Linzer Tart

- 1 cup all-purpose flour
- ¼ cup granulated sugar
- ¼ teaspoon baking powder
- ¼ teaspoon salt
- ¼ teaspoon ground cinnamon
- ¼ cup packed brown sugar
- 6 tablespoons butter
- 1 slightly beaten egg yolk
- ¼ cup finely chopped blanched almonds
- 2 tablespoons *each* of *six* fruit preserves and marmalades

Thoroughly stir together flour, sugar, baking powder, salt, and cinnamon. Stir in brown sugar. Cut in butter till mixture resembles coarse crumbs. Add egg yolk and almonds; mix thoroughly with hands till mixture forms a ball. Reserve ½ *cup* of the dough. Press remaining dough evenly onto bottom and about ½ inch up sides of an 8-inch flan pan *or* baking dish. Bake at 375° till brown, 12 to 15 minutes. Pinch off small amount of reserved dough; form into a ball; place in center of tart. Divide remaining dough into six parts. Roll each part into a 4-inch rope. Arrange spoke-fashion (starting from ball in center) to divide tart into six equal sections. Fill each section with two tablespoons of one of the preserves *or* marmalades, alternating different colors and flavors. Bake at 375° till golden, 12 to 15 minutes. Makes 6 servings.

Fruit Melange Pie

Line 9-inch pie plate with *half* of the **pastry for a 9-inch lattice-top pie.** Combine 1½ cups **sugar** and ⅓ cup all-purpose **flour.** Toss with 1½ cups diced fresh **pineapple,** 1½ cups diced fresh **rhubarb,** 1½ cups sliced **strawberries,** and 1 sliced **banana.** Turn fruit mixture into pastry-lined plate. Dot with 1 tablespoon **butter** *or* **margarine.** Adjust top crust using remaining pastry. Cut slits for escape of steam. Seal edges and make a high fluted edge. Bake at 400° till done, about 50 minutes.

Cherry-Raspberry Pie

        1 10-ounce package frozen
            red raspberries
        2 cups pitted fresh *or* frozen
            tart red cherries
        Pastry for 9-inch lattice-top
            pie
        ¾ cup sugar
        3 tablespoons cornstarch
        Red food coloring (optional)

Thaw frozen raspberries and cherries. Line 9-inch pie plate with *half* the pastry. Drain raspberries; *reserve* syrup. Add water to syrup to make 1 cup. Mix sugar, cornstarch, and ¼ teaspoon salt. Stir in reserved syrup; a few drops food coloring, if desired; and cherries. Cook and stir over low heat till thickened. Stir in raspberries. Pour mixture into pastry-lined pie plate. Adjust lattice top; seal. Crimp edge. Bake at 425°, 30 minutes.

Pineapple Pie

        Pastry for 2-crust 9-inch
            pie
        ¾ cup sugar
        3 tablespoons quick-cooking
            tapioca
        Dash salt
        4 cups fresh pineapple
            chunks
        ½ teaspoon grated lemon peel
        1 tablespoon lemon juice
        1 tablespoon butter *or* margarine

Line 9-inch pie plate with *half* of the pastry. In mixing bowl stir together sugar, tapioca, and salt. Add pineapple, lemon peel, and lemon juice. Let stand 15 minutes. Turn pineapple mixture into pastry-lined pie plate. Dot with butter *or* margarine. Adjust top crust; seal and crimp edges. Cut slits for *escape* of steam. Bake at 400° for 40 to 45 minutes.

Summertime is the season of family picnics and reunions. It's also the time for fresh cherries. Combine the two by bringing *Cherry-Raspberry Pie* to your next family gathering. If the occasion calls for a special gift, give your pie in a carrier or include a wooden pastry wheel with it.

Show-Off Garden Gifts

Make it harvest time all year round. Give gifts that preserve the garden goodness of fruits and vegetables.

You'll find this chapter full of garden gift ideas that will delight everyone on your gift list. For fruit fanciers in your crowd choose from brandied fruit, applesauce, cinnamon pears, and an assortment of fruit juices. For the hearty eaters there are vegetable soups—both hot and cold. For pickle lovers make everything from mustard pickles to zucchini relish to mango chutney. For those with a sweet tooth, try one of the jellies, jams, or preserves. The recipes on these pages are so good you'll want to show them off.

Add a personal touch to garden gifts. Give *Grapefruit-Orange Juice* in a basket with extra fruit. Pack *Fresh Mint Jelly* in glasses with decorative tops. Put *Low-Cal Strawberry-Pear Jam* in a papier-mâché strawberry and fill a papier-mâché cucumber with a jar of *Bread-and-Butter Pickles* (see Index for pages.)

Fruit and Vegetable Treasures

Brandied Fresh Fruit Pot

2½ cups granulated sugar
2½ cups packed brown sugar
2 cups sectioned oranges
2 cups chopped fresh pineapple
2 cups chopped, peeled pears
2 cups chopped, peeled peaches
2 cups quartered maraschino
  cherries *or* halved and
  seeded grapes
2 inches stick cinnamon, broken
1 pint apricot brandy (2 cups)

In large bowl mix sugars and fruits. Let stand 3 hours; stir once or twice. Tie cinnamon in cheesecloth; add to fruit mixture along with brandy. Cover loosely *or* pour into a jar and cover loosely. Let stand one week; stir once a day. Pack in pint containers. Cover; refrigerate. Makes 6 pints.

To keep starter going: Add 1 cup sugar and 2 cups chopped fruit to replace every 2 cups of fruit and syrup removed. If too much syrup forms, add 2 cups fruit and no sugar. To activate starter again let stand at room temperature for several days. If mixture will not be used within a week, store loosely covered in refrigerator.

Directions to pack with fresh fruit pot: Keep fruit mixture refrigerated. Serve alone or over ice cream or angel food cake.

Cinnamon Pears

Wash, peel, halve, and core 4 pounds small **pears.** Place in **water** containing **ascorbic acid color keeper.** In large saucepan mix 4 cups **water,** 1 cup **red cinnamon candies,** and ¾ cup **sugar.** Heat to boiling; stir occasionally to dissolve sugar. Drain pears; add *half at a time* to boiling syrup. Return to boiling; simmer just till tender, 1 to 2 minutes. Pack pears in hot, clean pint jars; leave ½-inch headspace. Cover with boiling syrup; leave ½-inch headspace. Adjust lids. Process in boiling water bath, 20 minutes. (Start timing when water returns to boiling.) Makes 4 or 5 pints.

Brandied Applesauce

7 pounds apples, cored and cut
  up (24 cups)
4 oranges, peeled and cut up
1½ to 2 cups sugar
½ cup peach *or* apple brandy
2 teaspoons pumpkin pie spice

In 10-quart kettle *or* Dutch oven mix apples, oranges, and 1 cup water. Cover and simmer till very tender, about 40 minutes, stirring down fruit occasionally. Press fruit through a food mill. Discard peels left in mill. Return fruit to kettle. Add sugar, as desired; brandy; and pumpkin pie spice. Boil gently, uncovered, 30 to 35 minutes, stirring often. Cool quickly by placing pan in bowl surrounded by ice water. Spoon into pint *or* quart freezer containers. Seal, label, and freeze. Makes 5 pints.

Directions to pack with applesauce: Keep frozen. To use, thaw.

Fruit Bowl

4 cups water
1 cup sugar
2 3-pound pineapples
2 pounds seedless green grapes
2 pounds fresh apricots

Mix water and sugar; boil 5 minutes. Skim surface, if necessary. Keep hot but not boiling. Remove crowns from pineapples. Peel and slice ½ inch thick. Remove eyes and core from each slice. Cut pineapple into chunks, reserving juice. Wash and drain grapes. Remove stems. Wash and drain apricots; halve and pit. Toss apricots with reserved pineapple juice. Simmer pineapple chunks in hot syrup till tender, 5 to 10 minutes. Add apricots to syrup with grapes. Simmer fruit till heated through, about 5 minutes. Pack hot fruit into hot, clean jars; leave 1-inch headspace. Cover with boiling syrup; leave ½-inch headspace. Adjust lids. Process in boiling water bath 20 minutes for pints *or* 25 minutes for quarts. (Start timing when water returns to boiling.) Makes 8 pints.

Best Tomato Catsup

1 cup white vinegar
1½ inches stick cinnamon, broken
1½ teaspoons whole cloves
1 teaspoon celery seed
8 pounds tomatoes (25 medium)
1 medium onion, chopped
¼ teaspoon cayenne
1 cup sugar
4 teaspoons salt

Mix vinegar, cinnamon, cloves, and celery seed. Cover; bring to boiling. Remove from heat; let stand. Wash, core, and quarter tomatoes. Let stand in colander to drain. Place in a large kettle. Add onion and cayenne. Bring to boil; cook 15 minutes. Stir often. Put tomatoes through food mill; discard seeds and skins. Add sugar to tomato juice. Bring to boil; simmer till reduced by half, 1½ to 2 hours (measure depth with ruler at start and end). Strain vinegar mixture into tomatoes; discard spices. Add salt. Simmer till desired consistency, about 30 minutes. Stir often. Pour hot catsup into hot, clean pint jars; leave ½-inch headspace. Adjust lids. Process in boiling water bath 5 minutes. (Start timing when water returns to boiling.) Makes 2 pints.

Tomato Paste

Wash, core, and cut up 40 pounds **tomatoes** (about 17 quarts); drain off excess liquid by pressing tomatoes *gently* against the sides of a colander (about 15 cups will drain off). Divide drained tomatoes and 2½ cups chopped **sweet red peppers** between two 8- to 10-quart kettles *or* Dutch ovens. Bring to boiling; reduce heat. Boil gently, uncovered, for 1 hour, stirring occasionally. Put mixture through food mill; return purée to kettles and discard skins and seeds. Add 2 **bay leaves** and 2 teaspoons **salt** to *each* kettle. Continue boiling, uncovered, for 1 hour.

Combine the mixtures in one kettle. Continue boiling till mixture is thick enough to round up on a spoon, 1 to 1½ hours more. Stir often during last 30 minutes. Discard bay leaves. Pour tomato mixture into hot, clean half-pint jars; leave ½-inch headspace. Adjust lids. Process in boiling water bath 45 minutes. (Start timing when water returns to boiling.) Makes 8.

Gazpacho

6 very ripe tomatoes, peeled
  and chopped (3 cups)
1 medium cucumber, peeled,
  seeded, and chopped (1 cup)
½ cup finely chopped onion
½ cup finely chopped green pepper
1 small clove garlic, minced
1½ cups tomato juice
¼ cup olive oil
2 tablespoons vinegar
1 teaspoon salt
  Few drops bottled hot pepper
  sauce.

In bowl mix tomato, cucumber, onion, green pepper, and garlic. Mix tomato juice, oil, vinegar, salt, pepper sauce, and ⅛ teaspoon pepper. Pour over vegetables. Mix well. Chill. Spoon into pint containers. Seal, label, and refrigerate. Makes about 3 pints.

Directions to pack with soup: Soup will keep several days in refrigerator. Serve cold.

Carrot Vichyssoise

5 leeks, thinly sliced
  (¾ cup)
1 medium onion, thinly sliced
½ cup thinly sliced celery
2 tablespoons butter *or*
  margarine
4 cups sliced, peeled potatoes
2 cups chicken broth
½ teaspoon salt
2 cups shredded carrots
  (5 medium)
1½ cups light cream
1 cup milk

Cook leeks, onion, and celery in butter till tender. Add potatoes, broth, and ½ teaspoon salt. Cook 25 to 30 minutes. Meanwhile, place carrots in ½ cup boiling salted water. Cover; simmer 6 to 8 minutes. Drain. Rub leek mixture through fine sieve or puree in blender. Add light cream, milk, and drained carrots. Season to taste with salt and pepper. Chill. Spoon into pint containers. Seal, label, and refrigerate. Makes 4 pints.

Directions to pack with soup: Soup will keep several days in refrigerator. Serve cold.

Bean and Vegetable Soup

      8 cups cold water
   1¼ cups dry navy beans
      2 tablespoons instant beef
         bouillon granules
      1 teaspoon sugar
      1 teaspoon dried thyme, crushed
      1 large bay leaf
      1 28-ounce can tomatoes, cut up
      1 cup chopped onion
      ½ cup sliced carrot
      ½ cup chopped celery
      1 cup tiny shell macaroni
      1 8-ounce can peas
      1 8-ounce can whole kernel corn

In 4-quart Dutch oven mix water and beans. Bring to boiling; simmer 2 minutes. Remove from heat. Cover; let stand 1 hour. Add bouillon, sugar, thyme, bay leaf, ½ teaspoon salt, and ⅛ teaspoon pepper. Bring to boiling; cover. Reduce heat; simmer 1 hour. Add tomatoes, onion, carrot, and celery. Cover; simmer 20 minutes. Add macaroni; cook 10 minutes. Remove bay leaf. Stir in undrained peas and corn. Spoon into quart freezer containers; leave ½-inch headspace. Cool. Seal, label, and freeze. Makes about 3 quarts.

Directions to pack with soup: Keep frozen till ready to use. Heat one 4-cup portion frozen soup, covered, over medium heat till hot, 30 minutes. Stir often to break up soup.

Beef Soup Stock

Have butcher break up 4 pounds **beef shanks and bones.** Place shanks and bones; 1 large **onion,** cut in wedges; 3 **carrots,** cut in 1-inch pieces; and 3 stalks **celery with leaves** in roasting pan. Bake at 375°, stirring often, till meat is browned, 45 to 60 minutes. Transfer mixture to large kettle. Add 4 quarts **water;** 1 small **turnip,** cut in wedges; ¼ of small head **cabbage;** 1 tablespoon **salt;** 3 cloves **garlic;** 3 sprigs **parsley;** 10 **peppercorns;** and 2 **bay leaves.** Bring to boiling. Cover; simmer 3 hours. Cool. Strain; skim off fat. Chill. Remove remaining fat. Spoon into pint freezer containers; leave ½-inch headspace. Seal, label, and freeze. Makes 5 or 6.

Directions to pack with stock: Keep frozen. To use, thaw completely.

Creole Lima Soup

      8 cups cold water
   2½ cups dry lima beans
         (1 pound)
            • • •
      2 large ham hocks (1½ to 1¾
         pounds total)
      2 cups chopped onion
      ½ cup snipped parsley
      2 large bay leaves
   1½ teaspoons salt
      ⅛ teaspoon pepper
      2 13¾-ounce cans tomato juice
   1½ cups chopped carrot
      1 cup chopped green pepper
      2 teaspoons Worcestershire sauce
      ½ teaspoon chili powder
      ¼ teaspoon bottled hot pepper
         sauce
      1 10-ounce package frozen cut
         okra

In a 4- to 6-quart kettle *or* Dutch oven combine water and lima beans. Bring to a boil; simmer 2 minutes. Remove from heat. Cover; let stand 1 hour. Add ham hocks, onion, parsley, bay leaves, salt, and pepper. Simmer, covered, for 2 hours. Remove and discard bay leaves. Remove ham hocks. When cool enough to handle, remove meat from bones; cut into pieces. Set aside. Discard bones. Mash bean mixture slightly. Add ham pieces, tomato juice, carrot, green pepper, Worcestershire sauce, chili powder, and hot pepper sauce. Simmer, covered, till vegetables are tender, about 25 minutes. Stir in okra. Simmer 5 minutes longer. Divide mixture evenly among four quart freezer containers. Seal, label, and freeze. Makes about 4 quarts soup.

Directions to pack with soup: Keep frozen till ready to use. Heat one 4-cup portion frozen soup with ½ cup water, covered, over low heat till hot, about 40 minutes. Stir often to break up soup.

If there are some on your gift list who don't enjoy ▶ cooking, free them from cooking chores by giving them frozen cartons of homemade soup such as *Bean and Vegetable Soup.* Include a set of mugs to serve the soup in and enhance your gift.

Good Eating!

Tomato Juice Cocktail

8 pounds tomatoes
1 cup chopped celery
½ cup chopped onion
¼ cup lemon juice
1 tablespoon sugar
2 teaspoons salt
2 teaspoons prepared
    horseradish
2 teaspoons Worcestershire
    sauce
¼ teaspoon bottled hot pepper
    sauce

Thoroughly wash tomatoes and remove stem ends and cores, if present. Cut up tomatoes. (Should measure about 19 cups.) In 8- to 10-quart kettle *or* Dutch oven combine tomatoes, chopped celery, and onion. Cover and cook slowly until tomatoes are soft, about 15 minutes, stirring often. Press tomato mixture through food mill to extract juice. Measure 12 cups juice.

Boil tomato juice gently, uncovered, about 30 minutes; stir often. Add lemon juice, sugar, salt, horseradish, Worcestershire sauce, and bottled hot pepper sauce; simmer 10 minutes more. Pour hot tomato juice into hot, clean pint jars, leaving ½-inch headspace. Adjust lids. Process in boiling water bath 10 minutes. (Start timing when water returns to boiling.) Makes about 5 pints tomato juice.

Pineapple Juice

4 pineapples (about 2¾ pounds
    each)
¼ to ⅓ cup sugar

Wash pineapples; remove crowns. Peel pineapples and remove eyes. Place fruit through food chopper, using coarse blade. Measure about 8 cups. Pour into a 6- to 8-quart kettle *or* Dutch oven. Cover and boil 10 minutes. Strain hot juice through clean muslin *or* several thicknesses of cheesecloth.

When cool squeeze muslin to extract remaining juice. Strain juice again. Add sugar to desired sweetness. Heat juice and sugar till just boiling. Pour into hot, clean pint jars, leaving ½-inch headspace. Adjust lids. Process in boiling water bath 15 minutes. (Start timing when water returns to boiling.) Makes 2 pints.

Apple-Grape Juice

6 pounds apples
3 pounds Concord grapes
6 cups water
● ● ●
½ to ⅔ cup sugar

Wash, core, and coarsely chop apples. Wash and stem grapes. Measure 8 cups grapes. In 4- to 6-quart kettle *or* Dutch oven combine fruit and water. Bring to boiling; reduce heat. Cover; simmer 5 minutes. Mash fruit. Cook 5 minutes more. Strain through clean muslin *or* several layers of cheesecloth. Let juice stand 1 to 2 hours (*or* overnight) to let sediment settle. Pour off juice *being careful not to disturb sediment.* In Dutch oven heat juice to boiling. Stir in sugar to desired sweetness. Pour hot juice into hot, clean pint jars; leave ½-inch headspace. Adjust lids. Process in boiling water bath 15 minutes. (Start timing when water returns to boiling.) Makes 5 pints.

Grapefruit-Orange Juice

Tart juice fans will enjoy this breakfast drink pictured on pages 32-33—

Cut 24 medium **oranges** (10 pounds) and 5 or 6 large **grapefruit** in half. Extract and strain the juice from each type of fruit. Measure 8 cups of orange juice and 4 cups grapefruit juice. In large saucepan combine juices. Bring to boiling. Pour hot juice into hot, clean pint jars; leave ½-inch headspace. Adjust lids. Process in boiling water bath 20 minutes. (Start timing when water returns to boiling.) Makes 6 pints.

Apricot Nectar

Pit and slice 2 pounds fresh **apricots;** measure 6 cups fruit. In 8- to 10-quart kettle *or* Dutch oven combine apricots and 5 cups **water.** Cook till tender, 5 to 10 minutes. Press apricots through food mill. Measure about 7 cups purée; add 1 cup **sugar.** Heat and stir till sugar is dissolved and mixture is heated through. Pour into hot, clean pint jars; leave ½-inch headspace. Adjust lids. Process in boiling water bath 10 minutes. (Start timing when water returns to boiling.) Makes 4 pints.

Pickle and Relish Potpourri

Bread and Butter Pickles

Tasty pickle slices shown on pages 32-33—

16 cups sliced, unpeeled medium
    cucumbers
6 medium white onions,
    sliced (6 cups)
2 green peppers, sliced
3 cloves garlic, scored
⅓ cup pickling salt
    Cracked ice
5 cups sugar
3 cups cider vinegar
2 tablespoons mustard seed
1½ teaspoons celery seed
1½ teaspoons ground turmeric

Combine cucumber, onion, green pepper, and whole garlic cloves. Add salt; cover with cracked ice. Mix thoroughly. Let stand 3 hours; drain well. Discard garlic. Combine remaining ingredients; pour over cucumber mixture. Bring to boiling. Fill hot, clean pint jars with vegetables and liquid, leaving ½-inch headspace. Adjust lids. Process in boiling water bath 5 minutes for pints. (Start timing when water returns to boiling.) Makes 8 pints.

Quick Mustard Pickles

2½ to 3 pounds medium cucumbers
1½ cups vinegar
1 cup water
1 cup sugar
½ cup prepared mustard
2 teaspoons salt
1 teaspoon prepared horseradish

Wash cucumbers; cut in ½-inch chunks *or* ¼-inch slices. Measure 8 cups. Set aside. In large saucepan mix remaining ingredients. Bring to boil. Pack cucumbers into hot, clean pint jars; leave ½-inch headspace. Pour hot pickling liquid over cucumbers, leaving ½-inch headspace. (Liquid will be cloudy due to mustard.) Adjust lids. Process in boiling water bath 5 minutes. (Start timing when water returns to boiling.) Mustard settles on standing. Makes 4 pints.

Green Tomato Pickles

4 pounds green tomatoes
4 medium onions, sliced
1 cup chopped green pepper
8 cups white vinegar
5 cups sugar
¼ cup mustard seed
1 tablespoon celery seed
1 teaspoon ground turmeric

Wash and core tomatoes; slice ¼ inch thick. Measure 16 cups. Mix tomatoes, onions, and pepper; set aside. In saucepan mix remaining ingredients; bring to boil. Pack vegetables into hot, clean pint jars; leave ½-inch headspace. Pour hot liquid over tomatoes; leave ½-inch headspace. Adjust lids. Process in boiling water bath 15 minutes. (Start timing when water returns to boil.) Makes 8 pints.

Watermelon Pickles

2 pounds watermelon rind
4 cups water
¼ cup pickling salt
2 cups sugar
1 cup white vinegar
1 cup water
1 tablespoon broken stick
    cinnamon
1½ teaspoons whole cloves
½ lemon, thinly sliced

Trim dark green and pink parts from watermelon rind. Cut in 1-inch cubes; measure 7 cups. Mix 4 cups water and pickling salt; pour over rind (add more water, if necessary, to cover). Let stand overnight. Drain; rinse rind. Cover with cold water. Cook till tender; drain. Combine sugar, vinegar, 1 cup water, cinnamon, and cloves. Simmer 10 minutes; strain. Add drained rind and lemon to strained vinegar mixture. Simmer till rind is clear. Pack rind and syrup into hot, clean half-pint jars; leave ½-inch headspace. Adjust lids. Process in boiling water bath 5 minutes. (Start timing when water returns to boil.) Makes 5 half-pints.

Pickled Beets with Horseradish

    4 pounds small whole beets with
        tops
    2 small onions, sliced
            • • •
    3 cups water
    1 cup vinegar
    1 cup sugar
    ⅓ cup prepared horseradish
    1 tablespoon mixed pickling
        spices
    2 bay leaves, crushed
    1½ teaspoons salt
    1 teaspoon dry mustard
    ½ teaspoon whole cloves
    ½ teaspoon whole allspice

Wash beets. Remove tops, leaving 1-inch stems. Cook beets, covered, in boiling salted water till tender, about 25 minutes. Drain. Slip off skins; discard tops. Slice beets; measure 6 cups. Mix with onion; set aside. Combine 3 cups water, vinegar, sugar, horseradish, and seasonings. Cover; simmer 10 minutes. Pack sliced beets and onions in hot, clean half-pint jars, leaving ½-inch headspace. Pour hot pickling liquid over beets and onions; leaving ½-inch headspace. Adjust lids. Process in boiling water bath 30 minutes. (Start timing when water returns to boiling.) Makes 6 half-pints.

Dill Pickled Beans

    2 pounds green beans
    3 cups water
    1 cup white vinegar
    2 tablespoons pickling salt
    2 tablespoons dried dillweed
    ¼ teaspoon cayenne
    2 cloves garlic, minced

Wash beans; drain. Trim ends. Cut beans to fit pint jars. Cook beans in a large amount of boiling water, uncovered, for 3 minutes. Drain. Set aside. In 4- to 6-quart kettle *or* Dutch oven mix 3 cups water, vinegar, salt, dillweed, cayenne, and garlic; bring to boiling. Pack beans lengthwise into hot, clean pint jars; leave ½-inch headspace. Pour hot pickling liquid over beans; leave ½-inch headspace. Adjust lids. Process in boiling water bath 10 minutes. (Start timing when water returns to boil.) Makes 4.

Pickled Mushrooms

    1 pound whole mushrooms
            • • •
    2 medium onions, thinly sliced
        and separated into rings
    1½ cups red wine vinegar
    1½ cups water
    ½ cup packed brown sugar
    4 teaspoons pickling salt
    1 teaspoon dried tarragon,
        crushed

Thoroughly wash the mushrooms; trim stems. In 3-quart saucepan combine onion rings, red wine vinegar, water, brown sugar, pickling salt, and the tarragon; bring the mixture to boiling. Add the mushrooms; simmer, uncovered, 5 minutes. Lift the mushrooms and onion rings from the pickling liquid with slotted spoon. Reserve the liquid; keep hot.

Pack vegetables in hot, clean half-pint *or* pint jars, leaving ½-inch headspace. Cover with hot pickling liquid, leaving ½-inch headspace. Adjust lids. Process in boiling water bath 5 minutes for both half-pints and pints. (Start timing when water returns to boiling.) Makes 4 half-pints *or* 2 pints.

Curried Zucchini Pickles

    24 medium zucchini (7 pounds)
    ¼ cup pickling salt
            • • •
    3 cups sugar
    3 cups vinegar
    ⅓ cup mustard seed
    4 teaspoons celery seed
    1 tablespoon curry powder

Thoroughly wash zucchini and cut into 3-inch sticks *or* ¼-inch slices. Sprinkle with salt. Add cold water to cover. Let stand 3 hours. Drain and rinse with cold water. Drain well. In 10-quart kettle combine sugar, vinegar, mustard seed, celery seed, and curry. Bring to boiling. Add zucchini. Heat through, but do not boil, for about 5 minutes. Pack zucchini in hot, clean pint jars; leaving ½-inch headspace. Pour hot pickling liquid over zucchini; leave ½-inch headspace. Adjust lids. Process in boiling water bath 5 minutes. (Start timing when water returns to boiling.) Makes 9 pints.

Carrot Pickles

     3 pounds carrots
      • • •
     2 cups vinegar
1½ cups water
     1 cup sugar
     3 inches stick cinnamon, broken
     1 tablespoon mixed pickling
          spices

Peel carrots; cut into 3-inch sticks. Cook in a large amount boiling water, covered, 15 to 20 minutes. Drain. Meanwhile, in large saucepan mix vinegar, 1½ cups water, sugar, and 1 teaspoon salt. Tie spices in cheesecloth bag; add to vinegar mixture. Boil 5 minutes. Pack carrots into hot, clean half-pint jars; leave ½-inch headspace. Remove spices from vinegar mixture. Pour boiling mixture over carrots; leave ½-inch headspace. Adjust lids. Process in boiling water bath 30 minutes. (Start timing after water returns to boiling.) Makes 6 half-pints.

Spicy Corn and Tomato Relish

     ½ cup sugar
     1 tablespoon ground turmeric
     2 17-ounce cans whole kernel
          corn, drained
     1 16-ounce can tomatoes, cut up
     2 cups chopped onion
     2 cups chopped, peeled cucumber
     2 cups chopped green pepper
     1 cup chopped celery
     1 cup vinegar
     2 teaspoons mustard seed
     ¼ teaspoon dried hot red pepper,
          crushed
      • • •
     2 tablespoons cornstarch

In 8- to 10-quart kettle mix sugar, turmeric, and 2 tablespoons salt. Add next nine ingredients. Bring to boiling; reduce heat. Simmer, uncovered, 30 minutes, stirring occasionally. Stir ¼ cup cold water into cornstarch; blend well. Add to vegetable mixture. Cook and stir till slightly thickened, about 3 minutes. Pack hot relish into hot, clean half-pint jars; leave ½-inch headspace. Adjust lids. Process in boiling water bath 15 minutes. (Start timing after water returns to boiling.) Makes 8 half-pints.

Pineapple Pickles

     2 medium pineapples
     2 cups packed brown sugar
     1 cup vinegar
     2 tablespoons whole cloves
     3 inches stick cinnamon, broken

Peel pineapples; core. Cut into 1-inch cubes or spears. In kettle mix sugar, vinegar, and 2 cups water. Tie spices in cheesecloth; add to mixture. Boil 5 to 8 minutes. Add pineapple. Cover; simmer 5 minutes. Remove spice bag. Pack pineapple into hot, clean half-pint jars; leave ½-inch headspace. Pour hot syrup over fruit; leave ½-inch headspace. Adjust lids. Process in boiling water bath 15 minutes. (Start timing when water returns to boil.) Makes 6.

Dress-up jars of *Spicy Corn and Tomato Relish* and *Pickled Mushrooms* by topping them with paper-maché mushrooms or turning them into corn ears.

For an economical gift that will truly be appreciated, combine jars of tangy *Cranberry-Orange Relish* with colorfully decorated kitchen utensils.

Cranberry-Orange Relish

   8 cups fresh cranberries
      (2 pounds)
   4 cups sugar
1½ cups water
   2 teaspoons grated orange peel
1½ cups orange juice
   ½ cup slivered almonds (optional)

In 6- to 8-quart kettle *or* Dutch oven mix cranberries, sugar, water, orange peel, and orange juice. Bring to boiling. Cook, uncovered, till cranberry skins pop, about 5 minutes, stirring once or twice. Stir in almonds, if desired. Remove from heat. Ladle hot relish into hot, clean half-pint jars, leaving ½-inch headspace. Adjust lids. Process in boiling water bath 5 minutes. (Start timing when water returns to boiling.) Makes about 8 half-pints.

Cranberry Catsup

   4 cups fresh cranberries
      (1 pound)
   2 cups finely chopped onion
   2 cups water
         • • •
   4 cups sugar
   2 cups white vinegar
   1 tablespoon salt
   1 tablespoon ground cinnamon
   1 tablespoon ground allspice
   1 tablespoon celery seed
   2 teaspoons ground cloves
   1 teaspoon pepper

In 3-quart Dutch oven *or* saucepan combine cranberries, onion, and water. Bring to boiling. Cover. Simmer till berries are easily mashed, about 10 minutes. Puree cranberry mixture in blender or push through sieve. In Dutch oven *or* saucepan combine cranberry purée, sugar, vinegar, salt, cinnamon, allspice, celery seed, cloves, and pepper. Bring to boiling. Boil gently, uncovered, till mixture is the consistency of catsup, 30 to 35 minutes, stirring occasionally. (Catsup will thicken on cooling.) Remove from heat; skim off foam with metal spoon. Ladle hot catsup into hot, clean pint jars, leaving ½-inch headspace. Adjust lids. Process in boiling water bath 5 minutes. (Start timing when water returns to boiling.) Makes 2 pints relish.

Spiced Gooseberry Relish

Wash and stem 8 cups **gooseberries**. In a large saucepan *or* Dutch oven combine stemmed gooseberries, 1½ cups **granulated sugar**, 1½ cups packed **brown sugar**, ½ cup **vinegar**, ½ cup **water**, ½ teaspoon ground **cloves**, ½ teaspoon ground **allspice**, ¼ teaspoon ground **cinnamon**, and dash **salt**. Cook over medium heat till thickened and bubbly, 25 to 30 minutes, stirring frequently. Spoon hot gooseberry relish into hot, clean half-pint jars; leave ½-inch headspace. Adjust lids. Process in boiling water bath 5 minutes. (Start timing when water returns to boiling.) Makes 5 half-pints.

Fruited Tomato Relish

  30 large tomatoes, peeled and
      chopped (15 cups)
4½ cups chopped, peeled pears
      (6 medium)
  4 cups chopped, peeled peaches
      (6 medium)
1½ cups chopped onion
1½ cups chopped celery
  3 cups sugar
  3 cups vinegar
  2 tablespoons salt
  2 tablespoons mixed pickling
      spices

Drain tomatoes well. In large kettle *or* Dutch oven mix tomatoes with pears, peaches, onion, and celery. Combine sugar, vinegar, and salt. Stir into tomato mixture. Tie pickling spices in cheesecloth bag; add to mixture. Boil gently, uncovered, 2 hours, stirring occasionally. Remove spice bag. Pour hot relish into hot, clean pint jars; leave ½-inch headspace. Adjust lids. Process in boiling water bath 5 minutes. (Start timing when water returns to boil.) Makes 8.

Sweet Frankfurter Relish

2 medium carrots
2 medium tomatoes, peeled and
    quartered
1 medium cucumber, seeded and
    quartered
1 medium onion, quartered
2 cups sugar
2 cups vinegar
½ teaspoon salt
⅛ teaspoon cayenne
1 tablespoon mixed pickling
    spices

Put carrots, tomatoes, cucumber, and onion through coarse blade of food grinder. Drain excess liquid. In large saucepan mix vegetables, sugar, vinegar, salt, and cayenne. Tie pickling spices in cheesecloth bag; add to saucepan. Bring to boiling. Cook over medium-high heat 45 to 50 minutes, stirring occasionally. Remove spice bag. Pour into hot, clean half-pint jars; leave ½-inch headspace. Adjust lids. Process in boiling water bath 5 minutes. (Start timing when water returns to boil.) Makes 2 half-pints.

Beet-Apple Relish

  6 cups cooked, peeled beets, cut
      up (4 pounds)
  6 large apples, peeled, cored,
      and quartered
  2 large onions, cut up
  4 inches stick cinnamon, broken
1½ cups sugar
1½ cups vinegar
  1 tablespoon salt

Put beets, apples, and onions through food grinder, using coarse blade. In large kettle *or* Dutch oven mix ground mixture, cinnamon, sugar, vinegar, salt, and ½ cup water. Bring to boiling. Cover; simmer 20 minutes, stirring often. Remove cinnamon. Ladle hot relish into hot, clean half-pint jars; leave ½-inch headspace. Adjust lids. Process in boiling water bath 15 minutes. (Start timing when water returns to boiling.) Makes 11 half-pints.

Louisiana Relish

  10 medium ears corn
   4 large onions
   2 large green peppers, halved
   2 sweet red peppers, halved
   2 medium cucumbers
   4 stalks celery
   1 small head cabbage
   2 small dried hot red peppers
   1 clove garlic
   ¼ cup pickling salt
2½ cups packed brown sugar
   2 tablespoons all-purpose flour
   3 cups vinegar

Remove husks and silks from corn. Rinse and cut corn from cobs. Set aside. Using coarse blade of food grinder, grind onions, peppers, cucumbers, celery, cabbage, dried peppers, and garlic. In large bowl mix ground vegetables with corn. Stir in pickling salt; cover. Let stand overnight. Rinse and drain. Combine brown sugar and flour; stir in vinegar and ½ cup water. Pour over vegetables. Bring mixture to boiling; boil gently 5 minutes. Ladle hot mixture into hot, clean pint jars, leaving ½-inch headspace. Adjust lids. Process in boiling water bath 15 minutes. (Start timing when water returns to boiling.) Makes 6 pints.

Apple-Grape Relish

Peel, core, and dice 3 pounds tart **apples** (9 medium). Place in 6-quart kettle *or* Dutch oven with 1 cup unsweetened bottled **grape juice,** 1 cup **vinegar,** and ½ teaspoon **salt.** Tie 3 tablespoons mixed **pickling spices** in cheesecloth bag. Add to mixture; stir. Bring to boiling; reduce heat. Boil gently, uncovered, till mixture is thick as applesauce, 15 to 20 minutes; stir often. Add 3 cups **sugar.** Cook 20 to 25 minutes; stir often. Remove spice bag. Ladle into hot, clean half-pint jars. Adjust lids. Process in boiling water bath 10 minutes. (Start timing when water returns to boil.) Makes 5 or 6 half-pints.

Carrot Chutney

    4 pounds carrots, peeled and
        sliced (24 medium)
    2 medium oranges
    1 lemon
    2½ cups sugar
    1⅓ cups vinegar
    2 tablespoons mixed pickling
        spices
    1 cup flaked coconut
    ½ cup raisins
    1 tablespoon grated fresh
        ginger root
    ½ teaspoon bottled hot pepper
        sauce

Cook carrots in boiling water to cover till very tender, 35 to 40 minutes. Drain and mash. (Measure about 5 cups.) Peel oranges and lemon. Reserve peel of *one* orange and *half* of the one lemon peel. Remove excess white membrane from reserved peels. Cut peel into very thin strips. Seed and thinly slice oranges and lemon. In 6-to 8-quart kettle mix sugar, vinegar, and peels. Place pickling spices in cheesecloth bag. Add bag to kettle. Bring mixture to boil; reduce heat. Cover; boil gently 5 minutes. Add carrots, orange and lemon slices, coconut, raisins, ginger root, and pepper sauce. Cook, uncovered, over medium heat till thickened, about 30 minutes; stir often. Discard spice bag. Ladle into hot, clean half-pint jars; leave ½-inch headspace. Adjust lids. Process in boiling water bath 10 minutes. (Start timing when water returns to boil.) Makes 8 or 9.

Mango Chutney

    1 green pepper, chopped
    1 small lemon, quartered and
        very thinly sliced
    1 cup vinegar
    ¾ cup sugar
    ½ cup chopped onion
    ¼ cup raisins
    1 clove garlic, minced
    ¾ teaspoon ground cinnamon
    ¼ teaspoon salt
    ¼ teaspoon ground cloves
    ¼ teaspoon ground allspice
    ⅛ teaspoon cayenne
            ● ● ●
    3 pounds mangoes, peeled and
        sliced (6 cups)
    2 large apples, peeled, cored,
        and sliced (2 cups)

In a large kettle *or* Dutch oven combine green pepper, lemon, vinegar, sugar, onion, raisins, garlic, cinnamon, salt, cloves, allspice, and cayenne. Bring mixture to boiling. Reduce heat and simmer, uncovered, 15 minutes, stirring frequently. Add sliced mangoes and apples. Simmer, uncovered, till fruit is tender, about 15 minutes, stirring occasionally. Ladle into hot, clean pint jars, leaving ½-inch headspace. Adjust lids. Process in boiling water bath 5 minutes. (Start timing when water returns to boiling.) Makes 3 pints.

Zucchini Relish

Grind 4 to 4½ pounds **zucchini,** cut up; 2 medium **onions,** cut up; and 1 **sweet red pepper,** cut up, in food chopper, using coarse blade. Add 2 tablespoons **salt.** Cover; refrigerate overnight. Drain; rinse in cold water. Drain well. In 4- to 5-quart kettle *or* Dutch oven combine zucchini mixture, 2 cups **sugar,** 1 cup **vinegar,** 1 cup **water,** 2 teaspoons **celery seed,** 1 teaspoon ground **turmeric,** 1 teaspoon ground **nutmeg,** and ⅛ teaspoon **pepper.** Bring mixture to boiling. Cover; boil gently for 10 minutes, stirring frequently. Ladle zucchini mixture into hot, clean pint jars, leaving ½-inch headspace. Adjust lids. Process in boiling water bath 15 minutes. (Start timing when water returns to boil.) Makes 4 pints.

Showcase Jellies and Jams

Easy Cranberry-Apple Jelly

In large kettle combine 3½ cups **cranberry-apple juice drink** and one 1¾-ounce package **powdered fruit pectin**. Cook and stir to boiling. Stir in 4 cups **sugar** immediately. Bring to full rolling boil; boil hard 2 minutes, stirring constantly. Remove from heat. Stir in ¼ cup **lemon juice.** Skim off foam. Pour into hot, sterilized jelly jars *or* glasses. Seal (*see page 89*). Makes 6.

Freezer Grape Jelly

    2 pounds Concord grapes
    4 cups sugar
    ½ of 6-ounce bottle liquid fruit
        pectin
    ¼ cup lemon juice

Wash and crush grapes. Strain juice through jelly bag *or* cheesecloth. Let stand overnight. Strain juice again, discarding any solids. Measure 2 cups juice (add water to make 2 cups, if necessary) *or* use 2 cups bottled unsweetened grape juice. Stir in sugar. Mix pectin and lemon juice. Stir into grape mixture. Stir 3 minutes. Pour at once into clean freezer containers (*or* into hot, sterilized half-pint jars *or* glasses, see page 89); seal. Cover; let stand at room temperature 24 hours. Store in refrigerator or freezer. Makes 5 or 6 half-pints.

Directions to pack with jelly: Store up to 6 weeks in refrigerator *or* 1 year in freezer.

Snowdrift Paraffin

Trim jellies with this topper shown on page 46 —

First seal jelly or jam with ⅛-inch hot **paraffin** (*see page 89*). Then melt 2 additional bars **paraffin** in top of double boiler over boiling water. Cool till paraffin becomes cloudy and starts to solidify. Quickly whip with electric mixer till foamy and slightly stiff. Work fast. (If paraffin solidifies, remelt and start again.) Spoon foamy paraffin over layer of hard paraffin. Cool till set. Covers 6 glasses.

Sangria Jelly

    1½ cups burgundy
    ¼ cup orange juice
    2 tablespoons lemon juice
    2 tablespoons orange liqueur
    3 cups sugar
        • • •
    ½ of 6-ounce bottle liquid
        fruit pectin

Combine wine, juices, and liqueur in top of double boiler. Stir in sugar. Place over, but not touching, boiling water and stir till sugar is dissolved, about 3 to 4 minutes. Remove from heat. At once, stir in fruit pectin and mix well. Skim off foam. Place metal spoon in hot, sterilized wine glass to prevent glass from breaking. Fill with hot syrup to within ⅛ inch from top of glass. Remove spoon. Repeat with remaining glasses. Seal with hot paraffin (*see page 89*). Makes 4.

Pepper Jelly

    2 pounds sweet red *or* green
        peppers (6 medium)
    2 or 3 large hot red peppers
    6½ cups sugar
    1 cup vinegar
    ½ cup water
    1 6-ounce bottle liquid fruit
        pectin
    Green *or* red food coloring
        (optional)

Put sweet red *or* green peppers through food grinder, using coarse blade. Reserve juice. Drain pulp well. Strain juice through cheesecloth. Repeat with hot red peppers. In large saucepan mix *1½ cups* sweet red pepper juice and *¼ cup* hot pepper juice. Add sugar, vinegar, and water. Bring to boil; add pectin. Boil vigorously 1 minute. Remove from heat; let stand 5 minutes. Add few drops green *or* red food coloring, if desired. Skim foam. Pour into hot, sterilized jelly jars *or* glasses. Seal (*see page 89*). Makes 8 half-pints.

Wine Jelly

A festive jelly shown on pages 86-87 —

>   3 cups sugar
>   2 cups wine
>   ½ of 6-ounce bottle liquid fruit
>   pectin
>   Snowdrift Paraffin (optional)
>   (see recipe, page 45)

Measure sugar and wine into top of double boiler; mix well. Place over but not touching rapidly boiling water. Stir till sugar is dissolved, 3 to 4 minutes. Remove from heat. At once stir in fruit pectin and mix well. Skim off foam, if necessary. Place a metal spoon in a hot, sterilized wine glass (to prevent glass from breaking). Quickly pour hot jelly into glass to within ⅛ inch from top. Remove spoon. Cover at once with ⅛-inch hot paraffin (see page 89). Repeat with five more glasses. After paraffin on wine glasses has hardened, top with Snowdrift Paraffin, if desired. Makes 6 glasses.

Tropical Fruit Punch Jelly

>   1 6-ounce can frozen red Hawaiian
>   fruit punch concentrate
>   3¼ cups sugar
>   3 tablespoons lemon juice
>   • • •
>   ½ of 6-ounce bottle liquid fruit
>   pectin

Prepare punch concentrate according to can directions. In 8- or 10-quart kettle combine 1¾ cups of the prepared punch and sugar. Bring to full rolling boil; boil hard for 1 minute, stirring constantly. Remove from heat and stir in lemon juice. Stir in pectin; mix well. Quickly skim off foam with a metal spoon. Pour at once into hot, sterilized half-pint jars *or* glasses; seal (see page 89). Makes 4.

◀ **Add wine-flavor to a friend's table** with one of these jellies, and decorate the gift by topping it with *Snowdrift Paraffin* (see recipe, page 45). Pictured clockwise from extreme left are *Honey-Orange Jelly* and variations of *Wine Jelly* flavored with sherry, rosé, Concord grape wine, apple wine, strawberry wine, and burgundy (in dessert dish).

Honey-Orange Jelly

>   1½ cups sauterne
>   2 teaspoons shredded orange peel
>   ½ cup orange juice
>   2 tablespoons lemon juice
>   2 tablespoons powdered fruit
>   pectin (½ of 1¾-ounce
>   package)
>   3 cups honey
>   • • •
>   Snowdrift Paraffin (optional)
>   (see recipe, page 45)

In large saucepan *or* Dutch oven mix sauterne, orange peel, orange juice, lemon juice, and fruit pectin. Bring to full rolling boil. Stir in honey; return to boiling. Boil 5 minutes, stirring constantly. Remove from heat. Skim off foam with metal spoon. Place a metal spoon in a hot sterilized wine glass. Quickly pour hot jelly into glass to ⅛ inch from top. Remove spoon. Cover with hot paraffin (see page 89). Repeat with five more glasses. After paraffin on glasses has hardened, top with Snowdrift Paraffin, if desired. Makes 6 glasses.

Fresh Mint Jelly

A flavorful accompaniment for lamb or other meats, pictured on pages 32-33 —

>   1½ cups mint leaves and stems,
>   loosely packed
>   2¼ cups water
>   2 tablespoons lemon juice
>   Green food coloring
>   3½ cups sugar
>   ½ of 6-ounce bottle liquid fruit
>   pectin

Wash mint leaves and stems. Place in saucepan with water. Bring to boiling. Remove from heat; cover. Let stand 10 minutes. Strain out mint leaves and stems, reserving 1¾ cups liquid. In a 4-quart kettle *or* Dutch oven combine mint liquid, lemon juice, and green food coloring. Stir in sugar. Bring mint mixture to full rolling boil. Stir in fruit pectin. Boil hard, uncovered, 1 minute, stirring constantly. Remove from heat. Quickly skim off foam with metal spoon. Pour hot jelly at once into hot, sterilized half-pint jars *or* glasses. Seal (see page 89). Makes about 3 half-pints.

Orange-Grapefruit Marmalade

    3 large grapefruit
    1 orange
    1 lime
    ¼ teaspoon baking soda
    5 cups sugar
    ½ of 6-ounce bottle liquid
        fruit pectin

Remove peels from grapefruit, orange, and lime. Scrape off excess white. Cut peels into fine strips. In saucepan combine the peels, baking soda, and 1½ cups water. Bring to boiling; cover. Simmer for 20 minutes. Meanwhile, remove white membrane from fruit. Section fruit, working over bowl to catch juices. Discard seeds. In 8- or 10-quart kettle or Dutch oven combine sections, juice, and undrained peel. Cover and simmer 10 minutes. Measure 3 cups cooked fruit mixture; add sugar and mix well. Bring to full rolling boil; boil, uncovered, for 1 minute. Remove marmalade from heat; stir in liquid fruit pectin. Skim off foam with metal spoon. Stir and skim for 10 minutes. Pour into hot, sterilized half-pint jars or glasses. Seal (see page 89). Makes 6 half-pints.

Tomato Marmalade

    1 medium orange, peeled and
        quartered
    2 pounds tomatoes, peeled, cored
        and chopped (4½ cups)
    2 tablespoons lemon juice
    3 inches stick cinnamon, broken
    2 teaspoons whole cloves
    5 cups sugar

Seed orange. Slice orange quarters crosswise very thinly over bowl to catch juice. In 5-quart kettle combine orange slices and juice, tomato, and lemon juice. Tie cinnamon and cloves in a cheesecloth bag. Add to tomato mixture. Bring mixture to boiling. Cover and simmer 10 minutes. Stir in sugar. Bring to full rolling boil; continue boiling and stirring till mixture sheets from metal spoon or till candy thermometer registers 220°, about 7 minutes. Remove marmalade from heat; remove bag of spices. Skim off foam with metal spoon. Pour at once into hot, sterilized half-pint jars or glasses. Seal (see page 89). Makes 6 half-pints.

Watermelon-Lemon Marmalade

    1 3-pound watermelon rind
    3 lemons
    1 1¾-ounce package powdered
        fruit pectin
    5 cups sugar

Trim dark green and pink parts from watermelon rind; cut rind into small chunks (measure about 6 cups). Grind with food grinder, using coarse blade. Measure 4 cups pulp including juices. Set aside.

Squeeze juice from lemons. Reserve peel of two of the lemons. Measure ½ cup lemon juice; set aside. Remove excess white from reserved lemon peels. Cut peel into very fine strips. Place lemon peel in 5-quart kettle. Cover with water; bring to boiling. Simmer 5 minutes. Drain, discarding cooking liquid. Add the 4 cups ground watermelon rind and liquid to peel in kettle. Cover; simmer 10 minutes, stirring frequently. Drain liquid. Measure and add water, if necessary, to make 2 cups. Return to kettle with rind and peel. Add lemon juice. Stir in pectin; bring to a full rolling boil. Add sugar at once. Bring to a full boil. Boil hard 1 minute, stirring constantly. Remove from heat. Skim off foam. Pour into hot, sterilized half-pint jars or glasses. Seal (see page 89). Makes 6.

Carrot-Raisin Honey

    1 medium orange
    1 large lemon
    2 cups shredded carrot (4 medium)
    2 cups water
    ¼ cup light raisins
        • • •
    5 cups sugar

Quarter orange and lemon. Remove seeds; thinly slice fruit with peel. In 8- to 10-quart kettle or Dutch oven combine orange and lemon slices, carrot, water, and raisins. Bring mixture to boiling. Reduce heat; simmer till carrot is tender, about 10 minutes. Add sugar. Bring to full rolling boil, stirring constantly. Continue cooking and stirring till mixture sheets from metal spoon, about 6 minutes. Remove from heat. Stir and skim off foam for 5 minutes. Pour into hot, sterilized half-pint jars or glasses; seal (see page 89). Makes 4 half-pints.

Fig-Lemon Jam

  2½ pounds fresh figs (13 figs)
    1 2x¼-inch strip lemon peel
   ½ cup light raisins
  7½ cups sugar
   ½ cup lemon juice
   ½ of 6-ounce bottle liquid
      fruit pectin

Wash figs; remove stem ends. Remove excess white from lemon peel. Grind figs, lemon peel, and raisins through food chopper; use coarse blade. Measure 4 cups fruit mixture into 8- to 10-quart Dutch oven. Add sugar and lemon juice; mix well. Bring to full rolling boil. Boil hard, uncovered, 1 minute; stir constantly. Remove from heat. Stir in pectin. Skim off foam. Pour into hot, sterilized pint jars *or* glasses; seal (*see* page 89). Makes 8 half-pints.

Gooseberry-Ginger Jam

  3 16-ounce cans gooseberries
  5 cups sugar
  1 teaspoon shredded orange peel
  1 teaspoon ground ginger
  ½ of 6-ounce bottle liquid
     fruit pectin

Drain berries; reserve syrup. Crush fruit; measure. Add enough reserved syrup to make 5½ cups. In 8- to 10-quart kettle mix fruit, sugar, peel, and ginger. Bring to full rolling boil. Boil hard, uncovered, 1 minute; stir constantly. Stir in pectin. Remove from heat. Skim off foam. Pour into hot, sterilized half-pint jars *or* glasses; seal (*see* page 89). Makes 7 half-pints.

Banana-Peach Jam

Peel, pit, and finely chop 7 medium **peaches.** Measure 3 cups. Slice 1 medium slightly green **banana.** Sprinkle with 3 tablespoons **lemon juice.** In 6- to 8-quart Dutch oven combine fruit with one 1¾-ounce package **powdered fruit pectin.** Bring to full rolling boil; stir constantly. Stir in 5½ cups **sugar.** Bring to full boil. Boil hard, uncovered, 1 minute, stirring constantly. Remove from heat. Skim off foam with metal spoon. Pour into hot, sterilized half-pint jars *or* glasses. Seal (*see* page 89). Makes 7.

Low-Cal Strawberry-Pear Jam

Both dieters and nondieters will enjoy this fresh-tasting jam pictured on pages 32-33 —

  2 cups strawberries,
    crushed
  3 medium pears, peeled, cored,
    and chopped (2 cups)
  1 cup water
  2 tablespoons lemon juice
    • • •
  1 1⅝-ounce package low-calorie
    strawberry-flavored gelatin
    (2 envelopes)
  Liquid artificial sweetener to
    equal ½ cup sugar

In medium saucepan combine crushed strawberries, chopped pears, water, and lemon juice. Cook and stir till fruit mixture comes to boiling. Stir in low-calorie gelatin. Return mixture to boiling, stirring constantly. Boil hard, uncovered, 1 minute, stirring constantly. Remove from heat; stir in artificial sweetener. Pour into hot, sterilized half-pint jars *or* glasses. Seal (*see* page 89). Refrigerate or freeze. Makes 4 half-pints.

  Directions to pack with jam: Store in refrigerator up to 6 weeks or in freezer for as long as 1 year.

Cherry-Nectarine Jam

    1 pound ripe tart red cherries
  1¼ pounds nectarines
    2 tablespoons lemon juice
    1 1¾-ounce package powdered
      fruit pectin
      • • •
    4 cups sugar

Sort, wash, and remove the stems from cherries. Pit and coarsely chop the cherries; measure 1½ cups. Pit and chop the nectarines; measure 2 cups. In 10-quart kettle *or* Dutch oven combine the chopped cherries and nectarines and lemon juice. Add the powdered fruit pectin to the mixture; mix thoroughly. Bring mixture to full rolling boil. Stir in sugar. Bring again to full rolling boil, stirring constantly. Boil hard, uncovered, 1 minute. Remove from heat; skim off foam with metal spoon. Pour hot jam into hot, sterilized half-pint jars *or* glasses. Seal (*see* page 89). Makes 5 half-pints.

Peach Butter

4½ to 5 pounds peaches, peeled and
  pitted (18 medium)
3 cups water
• • •
4 cups sugar
1 teaspoon ground cinnamon
½ teaspoon ground nutmeg

Chop peaches (measure about 11 cups). In an 8- to 10-quart kettle *or* Dutch oven combine chopped peaches and water. Cook fruit mixture, covered, on low heat till peaches are tender, about 40 minutes. Press fruit mixture through food mill *or* sieve. Return to kettle. Add sugar, cinnamon, and nutmeg. Bring to boiling. Boil gently, uncovered, until mixture is desired consistency, 40 to 45 minutes, stirring frequently. Carefully ladle hot butter into hot, clean half-pint jars, leaving ½-inch headspace. Adjust lids. Process in boiling water bath 10 minutes. (Start timing when water returns to boiling.) Makes 7 half-pints.

Dark corn syrup gives *Cinnamon-Apple Butter* its rich color. This flavorful spread complements all types of breads, especially baking powder biscuits.

Winter Squash Butter

6 to 6½ pounds acorn *or* other
  winter squash (4 large)
3 cups packed brown sugar
1 teaspoon grated lemon peel
¼ cup lemon juice
2 teaspoons ground cinnamon
1 teaspoon salt
1 teaspoon ground nutmeg

Halve squash; seed. In large kettle cook squash in small amount of boiling unsalted water, covered, till very tender, about 40 minutes. Drain; scoop out pulp. In large mixing bowl whip pulp till smooth using electric mixer. Measure 6 cups. In large kettle mix pulp, sugar, lemon peel and juice, cinnamon, salt, and nutmeg. Cook and stir till mixture boils. Consistency should be like apple butter. Boil a few minutes more, if necessary. Ladle into hot, clean half-pint jars; leave ½ inch headspace. Adjust lids. Process in boiling water bath 10 minutes. (Start timing when water returns to boiling.) Makes 8 half-pints.

Cinnamon-Apple Butter

10 pounds tart apples
5 cups apple cider *or* water
4 cups sugar
1 cup dark corn syrup
• • •
2 teaspoons ground cinnamon
¼ teaspoon ground cloves

Core and thickly slice the apples. (Measure 30 cups sliced.) Place apple slices in 10-quart kettle *or* Dutch oven. Add apple cider *or* water. Bring mixture to boiling; reduce heat. Cover and simmer till apples are tender, about 30 minutes, stirring occasionally. Press through food mill or sieve. Return to kettle. Boil apple mixture gently, uncovered, 30 minutes, stirring occasionally. Stir in sugar and dark corn syrup. Boil gently, stirring frequently with a long-handled spoon, till mixture is of desired thickness, about 1¾ hours. Stir in cinnamon and cloves. Cook and stir apple butter 15 minutes more. Pour hot butter into hot, clean half-pint jars. Adjust lids. Process in boiling water bath 10 minutes. (Start timing when water returns to boiling.) Makes 11 or 12 half-pints.

Apple-Blueberry Conserve

3 pounds tart apples (10 to 11
    apples)
1½ pints blueberries
    (3 cups)
3 lemons
3 cups sugar
½ cup chopped blanched almonds

Peel, core, and finely chop apples. (Measure about 8 cups.) Sort, wash, and remove stems from blueberries. Crush; measure 2 cups.

Squeeze lemons to measure ½ cup juice; reserve peel from *one* lemon. Set juice aside. Remove excess white from reserved peel. Slice peel into very thin strips. Cover peel with water. Cook, uncovered, till peel is tender, about 10 minutes. Drain thoroughly.

In 8- to 10-quart *kettle or* Dutch oven combine apples, blueberries, drained lemon peel, lemon juice, and sugar. Bring mixture to full rolling boil. Boil, uncovered, till mixture is thick and sheets off metal spoon, about 15 minutes. Stir occasionally. Stir in almonds. Remove from heat. Skim off foam with metal spoon. Pour into hot, sterilized half-pint jars *or* glasses. Seal (*see* page 89). Makes 7 half-pints.

Sun Preserves

3 cups strawberries,
    halved
2 cups sugar
1 cup coarsely chopped pineapple
½ cup honey
2 tablespoons lemon juice

Mix strawberries, sugar, pineapple, honey, and lemon juice in saucepan. Heat to boiling. Boil hard, uncovered, 8 to 10 minutes; stir constantly. Divide mixture into two 13x9x2-inch baking dishes, making sure syrup is no more than ½ inch thick. Cover dishes with clear plastic wrap. Leave one edge open slightly for evaporation. Set dishes on table *or* rack in full sunlight. Let stand till the consistency of honey, 5 to 8 hours; stir *every* 2 hours. Ladle into hot, sterilized half-pint jars *or* glasses. Seal (*see* page 89). Cool. Refrigerate or freeze. Makes 4 half-pints.

Directions to pack with preserves: Refrigerate preserves up to three weeks *or* freeze up to three months.

Rhubarb Conserve

3 cups diced rhubarb (12 ounces)
1 cup sugar
1 cup light corn syrup
• • •
2 teaspoons grated orange
    peel
⅓ cup orange juice
1 teaspoon grated lemon peel
3 tablespoons lemon juice
⅓ cup chopped maraschino
    cherries
½ cup chopped walnuts

In 4-quart *kettle or* Dutch oven combine rhubarb, sugar, and corn syrup. Let stand 1 hour. Add orange peel and juice and lemon peel and juice. Mix thoroughly. Bring mixture to full rolling boil. Boil, uncovered, till syrup sheets from metal spoon *or* till candy thermometer registers 220°, about 12 to 15 minutes, stirring occasionally. Stir in maraschino cherries and chopped walnuts. Heat through. Remove from heat. Skim off foam with metal spoon. Pour conserve into hot, sterilized half-pint jars *or* glasses. Seal (*see* page 89). Makes 3 half-pints.

Mixed Fruit Conserve

3 cups peeled, pitted, and
    diced peaches (1½ pounds)
2 cups pitted red plums cut up
2 cups peeled, cored, and
    diced pears (1 pound)
1 cup seedless green grapes,
    halved
4 cups sugar
• • •
½ cup chopped blanched almonds
¼ cup lemon juice

In 10-quart *kettle or* Dutch oven combine peaches, plums, pears, and grapes. Stir in sugar. Cook and stir till sugar is dissolved. Bring fruit mixture to full rolling boil. Boil, uncovered, till syrup sheets from metal spoon *or* candy thermometer registers 220°, 12 to 15 minutes, stirring constantly. Stir in almonds and lemon juice. Remove from heat. Skim off foam with metal spoon. Pour hot conserve into hot, sterilized half-pint jars *or* glasses. Seal (*see* page 89). Makes 6 half-pints.

Gift-Givers' Favorites from the Pantry

Expand your ideas about gifts from the kitchen by trying some of the recipes in this gift-givers' pantry.

If you're partial to sweets, begin by making one of the tempting candies. Choose from fudges, divinity, taffy, brittles, and caramels. Then dare to be different with your own homemade butters, sauces, vinegars, or seasoning mixtures.

Finally when you're invited to a party, bring a hostess gift from the snack or beverage sections. Pretzels, nibble mixes, dips, cheese balls, beverages mixes, and homemade cordials—you'll find them all here.

It's easy to add sparkle to a gift by choosing the right container. Give *Soft Whole Wheat Pretzels* (top shelf) in a wooden canister. Dress up jars of *Pineapple Ice Cream Sauce* to resemble a cowboy or chef. Pack *Corn-Nut Snack* in a ham can that has been transformed into a ladybug. Pour *Peach Cordial* (bottom shelf) into an attractive decanter. Spoon *Strawberry Butter* into ceramic or glass condiment jars. Poke *Cinnamon Lollipops* into a bright shiny apple. Give *Brown Sugar Peanut Brittle* in a delicate candy dish (see Index for page numbers).

Candy Jubilee

Apple-Peanut Butter Fudge

Mix one 6-ounce package **semisweet chocolate pieces,** *half* of a 7- *or* 9- *or* 10-ounce jar **marshmallow creme,** ½ cup **peanut butter,** and 1 teaspoon **vanilla.** Set aside. In buttered heavy 2-quart saucepan mix 2 cups **sugar** and ⅔ cup **apple juice.** Cook and stir till sugar dissolves and mixture boils. Cook to soft-ball stage *or* till candy thermometer registers 240°; stir frequently. Remove from heat; quickly add marshmallow mixture. Stir just till blended. Pour into buttered 9x9x2-inch baking pan. Top fudge with **chopped peanuts,** if desired. Cool. Cut in squares. Makes 3 dozen (1½-inch) pieces.

Java Fudge

A coffee-flavored fudge shown on page 2—

   3 cups sugar
1½ cups light cream
   3 tablespoons light corn syrup
   2 tablespoons instant coffee
      crystals
   Dash salt
   2 tablespoons butter *or* margarine
   1 teaspoon vanilla

In buttered 3-quart saucepan bring first five ingredients to boil; stir constantly. Boil *without stirring* to thread stage *or* till candy thermometer registers 234°. Remove from heat. Add butter and vanilla. *Do not stir.* Cool to 110°. Beat till fudge starts to lose its gloss, 10 minutes. Pour into buttered 8x8x2-inch baking pan. Cool. Cut in squares. Makes 1¾ pounds.

No-Cook Fudge

Stir ½ cup **butter** *or* **margarine** into ⅓ cup **boiling water.** Stir till melted. Beat in 4½ cups sifted **powdered sugar,** ½ cup nonfat **dry milk powder,** ½ cup **unsweetened cocoa powder,** and dash **salt.** Pour into buttered 8x8x2-inch baking pan. Refrigerate several hours. Cut into squares. Makes 3 dozen (1-inch) pieces.

Almond Fudge

   3 cups sugar
   1 cup milk
   2 tablespoons light corn syrup
   3 tablespoons butter *or* margarine
   ½ teaspoon vanilla
   ¼ teaspoon almond extract
      • • •
   ½ cup coarsely chopped toasted
      almonds

In heavy 3-quart saucepan combine sugar, milk, corn syrup, and ¼ teaspoon salt. Cook and stir over medium heat till sugar is dissolved. Cook *without stirring* to soft-ball stage *or* till candy thermometer registers 236°. Remove from heat. Add butter. Do not stir. Cool *without stirring* to 110°. Add vanilla and almond extract. Beat vigorously till fudge stiffens and begins to lose its gloss. Quickly stir in almonds. Pour into a buttered 8x8x2-inch baking pan. Cool; cut into squares. Makes 3 dozen pieces.

Easy Opera Fudge

Give this pink and white candy, shown on page 26, on St. Valentine's Day—

Chop ⅓ cup **maraschino cherries** and drain on paper toweling. In saucepan combine two 3¼- *or* 3⅝-ounce packages *regular* **coconut cream pudding mix,** ½ cup melted **butter** *or* **margarine,** and ½ cup **milk.** Cook and stir till mixture boils. Boil for 1 minute, stirring constantly. Remove from heat. Stir in ½ teaspoon **vanilla;** beat in 4½ cups sifted **powdered sugar** till smooth. Stir in ½ cup chopped **walnuts** and drained cherries. Pour into buttered 10x6x2-inch baking dish. Garnish with **walnut halves.** Cut into squares when cool. Makes 32 pieces.

If those on your gift list crave something sweet, ▶
try presenting them with *Apple-Peanut Butter Fudge,*
Maple Sponge Candy (see recipe, page 59), or *Spicy*
Sherried Walnuts (see recipe, page 66).

Cranberry Fudge

A fresh tasting variation of opera fudge pictured on page 58—

 2 cups sugar
 ½ cup milk
 ½ cup light cream
 1 tablespoon light corn syrup
 ½ teaspoon salt
 1 tablespoon butter *or* margarine
 1 teaspoon vanilla
 ½ cup fresh cranberries, chopped

Butter the sides of heavy 2-quart saucepan. In pan combine sugar, milk, cream, corn syrup, and salt. Cook and stir over medium heat till mixture boils. Cook to soft-ball stage *or* till candy thermometer registers 238°. Immediately remove from heat and cool to lukewarm (110°) *without stirring*. Add butter *or* margarine and vanilla. Beat vigorously till mixture stiffens and starts to lose its gloss, about 5 minutes. Quickly stir in cranberries and spread in buttered 9x5x3-inch loaf pan. Score while warm. Cut into pieces when fudge is cool. Makes 2½-dozen (1½x1-inch) pieces.

Holiday Divinity

Candied fruit sparks up this perennial Christmas favorite pictured on page 2—

 2½ cups sugar
 ½ cup light corn syrup
 ½ cup water
 ¼ teaspoon salt
 2 egg whites
 1 teaspoon vanilla
 1 cup chopped walnuts
 ¼ cup chopped candied cherries
 ¼ cup chopped candied pineapple

In a heavy 2-quart saucepan combine sugar, corn syrup, water, and salt. Cook and stir till sugar is dissolved. Continue cooking *without stirring* to hard-ball stage *or* till candy thermometer registers 260°. Meanwhile, beat egg whites with an electric mixer till stiff but not dry. Gradually pour syrup over the egg whites, beating constantly at high speed of mixer. Add vanilla and beat till candy holds its shape, 4 to 5 minutes. Stir in walnuts, candied cherries, and candied pineapple. Quickly drop from a teaspoon onto waxed paper. Makes 48 pieces.

Peanut Butter Divinity

 2½ cups granulated sugar
 ½ cup light corn syrup
 ½ cup water
 2 egg whites
 ½ teaspoon vanilla
    Sifted powdered sugar
 ½ cup creamy peanut butter

In buttered 2-quart saucepan, mix granulated sugar, corn syrup, and water. Cook and stir over medium heat till mixture boils. Continue cooking *without stirring* to hard-ball stage *or* till candy thermometer registers 260°. Meanwhile, beat egg whites with electric mixer till stiff but not dry. Gradually pour hot syrup over egg whites, beating constantly at high speed of mixer. Add vanilla; beat till candy holds its shape, 4 to 5 minutes. On towel dusted generously with powdered sugar, quickly pat candy to 10x4-inch rectangle. Dust lightly with more powdered sugar. Using rolling pin dusted with powdered sugar, roll candy to 16x 6-inch rectangle. Spread peanut butter over candy to within ½ inch of *one* of the long sides. Roll up from opposite side, using towel to help roll. Wrap in towel; chill till firm, about 1 hour. Cut in half crosswise; wrap in waxed paper. Refrigerate. To serve cut in slices slightly more than ½ inch thick. Makes about 48 pieces.

Aunt Belle's Brown Candy

 3 cups sugar
 1 cup light cream
 ⅛ teaspoon baking soda
 ¼ cup butter *or* margarine
 ½ teaspoon vanilla
 1 cup broken pecans

In heavy skillet melt *1 cup* sugar over *low heat* till melted and caramel-colored; stir constantly. Pour *slowly* into large saucepan with remaining sugar and cream. Cook and stir till mixture reaches firm-ball stage *or* till candy thermometer registers 246°. Remove from heat; add soda. Stir vigorously. Add butter; cool 10 minutes. Add vanilla; beat till mixture stiffens and begins to lose its gloss, about 5 minutes. Blend in nuts. Spread in buttered 8x8x2-inch baking pan. Cut in squares when cool. Makes 3 dozen (1-inch) squares.

Buttermilk Pralines

When making these pralines, shown on page 2, be sure to stir the syrup constantly to prevent it from scorching—

2½ cups sugar
1 cup buttermilk
1 teaspoon baking soda
¼ teaspoon salt
¼ cup butter *or* margarine
1 teaspoon vanilla

• • •

2 cups pecan halves

Butter a heavy 4-quart saucepan. In pan combine sugar, buttermilk, baking soda, and salt. Bring mixture to boiling over medium heat, *stirring constantly* . Reduce heat. Cook and stir to soft-ball stage *or* till candy thermometer registers 234°, 10 to 15 minutes. Remove from heat. Add butter and vanilla. *Do not stir.* Cool about 5 minutes. Beat till mixture is smooth and slightly thickened, 2 to 3 minutes. Stir in pecan halves. Immediately drop from a tablespoon onto waxed paper. If mixture becomes too thick to drop, stir in a teaspoon or two of water. Cool. Makes 24 pieces.

Buttery Molasses Taffy

As you may need some help in pulling this taffy, turn the occasion into a party and have three or four friends in for a taffy pull—

2 cups sugar
1½ cups water
1 cup molasses
½ cup butter *or* margarine
¼ cup light corn syrup

Butter a heavy 3-quart saucepan. In pan combine sugar, water, molasses, butter *or* margarine, and corn syrup. Cook over low heat, stirring till sugar is dissolved. Bring to boiling; boil gently to hard-ball stage *or* till candy thermometer registers 266°. Pour onto buttered platter or shallow baking pan.

Cool till easy to handle, 10 to 15 minutes. Butter hands lightly and pull candy till light in color and difficult to pull. On countertop rub and twist candy into ropes, ½ inch in diameter; cut into 1-inch pieces. Wrap each piece individually in clear plastic wrap. Makes about 1½ pounds candy.

Cashew Brittle

A new variation of old-fashioned brittle, this candy is shown on page 58—

2 cups sugar
1 cup light corn syrup
1 cup butter *or* margarine
3 cups cashews (about 12 ounces)
1 teaspoon soda

In heavy 3-quart saucepan combine sugar, corn syrup, and ½ cup water. Cook and stir till sugar dissolves. Bring syrup to boiling; blend in butter *or* margarine. Stir frequently after mixture reaches the thread stage and candy thermometer registers 230°. Add cashews when temperature reaches soft-crack stage, 280°. Stir constantly till temperature reaches hard-crack stage, 300°. Remove from heat. Quickly stir in soda, mixing well. Pour onto two buttered baking sheets *or* two buttered 15½x10½x 1-inch baking pans. As the candy cools, stretch it by lifting and pulling with two forks from edges to make it thinner. Loosen candy from pans as soon as possible. Turn candy over; break in pieces. Makes 2½ pounds candy.

Brown Sugar Peanut Brittle

Brown sugar makes this brittle, shown on pages 2 and 52-53, special—

2 cups granulated sugar
1 cup packed brown sugar
½ cup corn syrup
½ cup water
¼ cup butter *or* margarine
2 cups raw Spanish peanuts
1 teaspoon baking soda

In heavy 3-quart saucepan combine sugars, corn syrup, water, and dash salt. Cook and stir till sugars dissolve. When syrup boils, blend in butter. Stir frequently after mixture reaches thread stage and candy thermometer registers 230°. Add peanuts when temperature reaches soft-crack stage, 280°. Stir constantly till temperature reaches hard-crack stage, 300°. Remove from heat. Quickly stir in soda; mix well. Pour onto two buttered baking sheets *or* two buttered 15½x10½x1-inch baking pans. As candy cools, stretch it by lifting and pulling with two forks from edges to make it thinner. Break into pieces when cool. Makes 2 pounds.

Walnut Caramels

1 cup butter *or* margarine
2¼ cups packed brown sugar
1 cup light corn syrup
2 cups light cream
½ cup chopped walnuts

Butter sides of heavy 5-quart Dutch oven. In pan melt butter *or* margarine. Add brown sugar and dash salt. Stir till thoroughly combined. Stir in corn syrup; mix well. Gradually add cream, stirring constantly. Cook and stir over medium heat till candy reaches firm-ball stage *or* till candy thermometer registers 245°, 30 to 35 minutes. Remove from heat. Place walnuts in bottom of buttered 9x9x2-inch baking pan. Pour syrup over nuts. Cool. Cut in squares. Makes 36 1½-inch squares (about 2 pounds).

Peanut Butter Bonbons

2 cups peanut butter
½ cup butter *or* margarine
4½ cups sifted powdered sugar
3 cups crisp rice cereal
1 6-ounce package butterscotch
    pieces (1 cup)
1 6-ounce package semisweet
    chocolate pieces (1 cup)

Melt peanut butter and butter. Mix sugar and rice cereal. Pour butter mixture over cereal mixture. Blend together with hands. Form into ½-inch balls. Chill till firm. Melt butterscotch pieces in top of double boiler over boiling water. Dip *half* the candies in coating; swirl tops. Place on waxed-paper-lined baking sheet. Chill till firm. Repeat melting and dipping process with chocolate pieces and remaining candies. Chill till firm. Makes 100.

◄ **Candies and cookies make great gifts** any time. Choose from (clockwise from lower left) *Puddin' Head Gingerbread Men* (see recipe, page 21), *Walnut Caramels, Cranberry Fudge* (see recipe, page 56), *Peanut Butter Bonbons, Kringla* (see recipe, page 21), *Cashew Brittle* (see recipe page 57), *Peanut Butter Swirls* (see recipe, page 20), *Christmas Candy Molds* (see recipe, page 60), and *Maple Shortbread Bars* (see recipe, page 16).

Liqueur-Flavored Wafers

¼ cup butter *or* margarine
⅓ cup green créme de menthe *or*
    coffee-flavored liqueur *or*
    dark créme de cacao *or*
    Galliano
1 package vanilla creamy-type
    frosting mix

Melt butter with liqueur over boiling water in top of double boiler. Add frosting mix; mix well. Cook and stir till smooth and glossy, about 5 minutes. Drop from teaspoon onto waxed paper, swirling tops of candies. If candy hardens, add a few drops warmed milk. Cool. Makes 6 dozen pieces (about 1 pound).

Maple Sponge Candy

Add glamour to an old-fashioned candy, shown on page 55, by giving it in a canister—

Combine 1 cup **maple-flavored syrup,** ½ cup **sugar,** and 2 teaspoons **white vinegar** in heavy 2-quart saucepan. Bring to boiling over medium heat. Stir till sugar dissolves. Continue cooking, *without stirring* to hard-crack stage *or* till candy thermometer registers 300°. Remove from heat. Quickly stir in 2 teaspoons **baking soda;** mix well. Immediately pour into buttered 9x9x2-inch baking pan. *Do not spread.* Cool; break into pieces. Makes about ½ pound.

Nut-Stuffed Figs

24 whole dried figs (1 12-ounce
    package)
1 cup orange juice
1 tablespoon grated lemon peel
1 tablespoon lemon juice
3 tablespoons sugar
24 pecan halves
    Sugar

Remove stem end from figs. Combine orange juice, lemon peel and juice, and 3 tablespoons sugar. Pour over figs in saucepan. Heat to boiling. Simmer, covered, till fruit is tender, about 45 minutes. Drain well; cool. Insert knife in stem end of each fig to form a pocket. Fill each with a pecan half. Roll figs in remaining sugar. Dry overnight. Makes 24.

Chocolate-Covered Cherries

60 maraschino cherries with stems
3 tablespoons butter *or* margarine,
    softened
3 tablespoons light corn syrup
¼ teaspoon salt
2 cups sifted powdered sugar
• • •
1½ pounds dipping chocolate *or*
    white chocolate
    (for coating candy)

Drain maraschino cherries thoroughly. Place on paper toweling. Combine butter *or* margarine, corn syrup, and salt. Stir in sifted powdered sugar. Knead sugar mixture till smooth. (Chill if mixture is too soft.)

Shape 1 teaspoon of the sugar mixture around each cherry. Place on a waxed-paper-lined baking sheet; chill.

In a small heavy saucepan melt chocolate, stirring constantly. *Do not add any liquid.* Holding cherries by stems, dip one at a time into chocolate. Spoon chocolate over cherries to coat. Place cherries on waxed-paper-lined baking sheet. Chill till chocolate is hardened. Store candy in a covered container in a cool place. Let candies ripen a week or two. Makes 60 chocolate-covered cherries.

Cinnamon Lollipops

Try these licking-good candies, shown on pages 52-53, as a decoration for your next children's party. Then give one to each guest to take home.

1¾ cups red cinnamon candies
    (14 ounces)
1 cup water
⅔ cup light corn syrup
Dash salt

In a buttered 2-quart saucepan mix cinnamon candies, water, corn syrup, and salt. Cook and stir till candies dissolve and mixture boils. Continue cooking, *without stirring,* to hard-crack stage *or* till candy thermometer registers 300°. Remove from heat. Arrange wooden skewers 4 inches apart on a buttered baking sheet. Drop hot syrup from tip of tablespoon over skewers to form 2- to 3-inch suckers. Cool till firm. Wrap each candy in clear plastic wrap, if desired. Makes 2½ to 3 dozen suckers.

Christmas Candy Molds

Dazzle your friends with this candy shown on page 58—

2 cups sugar
1 cup light corn syrup
¼ teaspoon peppermint oil *or*
    other flavoring oil
Food coloring
Nonstick vegetable coating

In buttered 2-quart saucepan mix sugar, syrup, and ⅔ cup water. Bring to boiling; stir constantly till sugar dissolves. Cook to hard-crack stage *or* till candy thermometer registers 300°. Remove from heat; add flavoring oil and coloring. Cool to 200°. Meanwhile, spray inside of plastic Christmas candle molds well with nonstick vegetable coating. Using wooden spoon, push cooled syrup into molds. Work fast. Cool till firm. Remove molds. Makes 1 cup syrup.

Candy Tree

Display hard candy on the tree shown on page 4—

Spray one 12-inch **plastic foam cone** (with 4½-inch base) with **red spray paint.** Let dry. Clip a little off the twisted ends of candy wrappers of 3 pounds mixed wrapped **hard candies.** Stick a steel **dressmaker pin** through one end of each wrapper and attach candy to cone, beginning at bottom and working in circles to the top. Place tree in a 4-inch-high compote or sherbet dish. Top with **red ribbon bow.**

Old-Time Chewy Popcorn Balls

A Halloween or Christmas treat of popcorn and a sugar syrup shown on page 4—

5 quarts popped corn
2 cups sugar
1½ cups water
½ cup light corn syrup
1 teaspoon vinegar
1 teaspoon vanilla

Keep popcorn hot in a 300° to 350° oven. In a buttered saucepan combine sugar, water, corn syrup, vinegar, and ½ teaspoon salt. Cook and stir to hard-ball stage *or* till candy thermometer registers 250°. Stir in vanilla. Slowly pour over hot popped corn. Stir just till mixed. Butter hands; shape into 3-inch balls. Makes 15.

Sauces, Seasonings, and Mixes

Strawberry Butter

Sample this butter shown on pages 52-53—

Thaw one 10-ounce package frozen **strawberries.** In blender container mix berries, 1 cup softened **butter,** and 1 cup sifted **powdered sugar.** Cover; blend at high speed till smooth. Stop blender often and push mixture toward blades with scraper. Pack in ½-cup containers. Refrigerate. Makes 2½ cups.

Directions to pack with butter: Keep refrigerated till ready to use.

Homemade Butter

With electric mixer beat 2 cups cold **whipping cream** till liquid separates, 8 to 10 minutes. (Decrease speed during last few minutes.) Drain. Rinse with cold water. Drain well. Add ¼ teaspoon **salt** and 10 drops **yellow food coloring.** Stir till salt and coloring are thoroughly blended in. Refrigerate. Makes 1 cup.

Directions to pack with butter. Keep refrigerated till ready to use.

Energy Butter

  ½ cup currants
  1 7-ounce jar dry-roasted cashews
  ¾ cup sesame seeds (4 ounces)
  ⅓ cup shelled sunflower seeds
  6 tablespoons cooking oil

Pour boiling water over currants to cover; let stand till cool. Drain. In blender container combine *one third* of the cashews, sesame seeds, and sunflower seeds. Cover and blend on low speed till finely chopped, stopping often to scrape sides of container. Add *2 tablespoons* of the oil; blend till pureed. Turn into mixing bowl. Repeat twice more with remaining cashews, seeds, and oil. Mix the three mixtures. Blend in ½ teaspoon salt and currants. Pack in ½-cup containers. Refrigerate. Makes 2 cups.

Directions to pack with butter: Keep refrigerated till ready to use.

Pineapple Ice Cream Sauce

Try this fresh-tasting sauce, shown on pages 52-53, in a sundae—

  3 to 4 large pineapples
  4 cups sugar
  1 cup light corn syrup
  1 teaspoon finely shredded lemon
    peel
  ¼ cup lemon juice

Remove crowns from pineapples; peel, remove eyes, and core. Dice pineapple; measure 12 cups. Place about *2 cups* in blender container. Cover; blend till finely chopped, stopping to scrape sides. Remove pureed pineapple. Repeat process till all diced pineapple is pureed. In 6- to 8-quart Dutch oven combine pineapple, sugar, and corn syrup. Bring to full boil. Reduce heat; boil gently, uncovered, till desired consistency, 25 to 30 minutes. Stir often to prevent sticking. Stir in lemon peel and juice. Pour hot sauce into hot, clean half-pint jars, leaving ½-inch headspace. Adjust lids. Process in boiling water bath 10 minutes. (Start timing when water returns to boiling.) Makes 10 half-pints.

Rum-Cinnamon Syrup

  1½ cups water
  8 inches stick cinnamon, broken
  3 cups light corn syrup
  1½ cups packed brown sugar
  ¼ teaspoon rum extract
        • • •
  6 pieces stick cinnamon (each 2
    to 3-inches long)

In saucepan combine water and broken stick cinnamon. Simmer, covered, for 15 minutes. Add corn syrup and brown sugar. Cook and stir till sugar is dissolved; bring to boiling. Stir in rum extract. Strain out broken cinnamon. Pour hot syrup into hot, clean half-pint jars, leaving ½-inch headspace. Add one piece of stick cinnamon to each jar. Adjust lids. Process in boiling water bath 10 minutes. (Start timing when water returns to boiling.) Makes 6 half pints.

Blueberry Syrup

Spice up your favorite ice cream with this versatile syrup or serve it with pancakes and waffles—

12 cups fresh blueberries

● ● ●

6 cups sugar
1 cup water
2 tablespoons lemon juice

Sort, wash, and remove any stems from blueberries. Put about *one third* of the blueberries at a time in blender container. Cover and blend thoroughly. Repeat twice. In a 5-quart kettle *or* Dutch oven combine blueberry pulp, sugar, water, and lemon juice. Bring sugar mixture to a full rolling boil. Reduce heat. Boil gently, uncovered, 10 minutes. Remove from heat. Skim off foam with a metal spoon. Pour hot syrup into hot, clean half-pint jars, leaving ½-inch headspace. Adjust lids. Process in boiling water bath 10 minutes. (Start timing when water returns to boiling.) Makes about 9 half-pints.

Delight your friends on moving day, with this palate-tickling *Mushroom Spaghetti Sauce* in a jar decorated with various shapes of pasta.

Mushroom Spaghetti Sauce

1 pound ground beef
¾ pound bulk Italian sausage
1 28-ounce can tomatoes, cut up
2 cups tomato juice
1 15-ounce can tomato sauce
1½ cups chianti
1 cup chopped onion
¾ cup chopped green pepper
1 tablespoon sugar
1½ teaspoons Worcestershire sauce
1 teaspoon salt
½ teaspoon chili powder
⅛ teaspoon pepper
2 cloves garlic, minced
3 bay leaves
1 6-ounce can sliced mushrooms
¾ cup all-purpose flour

In Dutch oven brown ground beef and sausage; drain well. Stir in undrained tomatoes, *1 cup* of the tomato juice, tomato sauce, chianti, onion, green pepper, sugar, Worcestershire, salt, chili powder, pepper, garlic, and bay leaves. Bring to boiling; reduce heat. Simmer, covered, 45 minutes, stirring occasionally. Remove bay leaves. Drain mushrooms, reserving liquid. Blend flour with reserved mushroom liquid and remaining 1 cup tomato juice. Stir into sauce along with mushrooms. Cook and stir till thickened. Pack into hot, clean pint jars; leave 1-inch headspace. Adjust lids. Process in pressure canner at 10 pounds pressure, 75 minutes, being sure to follow manufacturer's directions. Refrigerate any sauce not processed and use within a few days. Makes 6.

Directions to pack with sauce: Before serving, boil meat sauce, covered, *at least 10 minutes before tasting or using.*

Soy-Sherry Basting Sauce

Mix 2 cups **soy sauce;** 2 cups dry **sherry;** ¼ cup **cooking oil;** ¼ cup **dry mustard;** 6 cloves **garlic** minced; 4 teaspoons ground **ginger;** and 4 teaspoons dried **thyme,** crushed. Pack in 1-cup containers. Refrigerate. Makes 4 cups.

Directions to pack with basting sauce: Keep refrigerated till ready to use. Use as a basting sauce when barbecuing beef, pork, lamb, poultry, or seafood.

Sweet-Sour Barbecue Sauce

½ cup finely chopped celery
½ cup finely chopped green pepper
1 clove garlic, minced
¼ cup butter *or* margarine
2 cups catsup
2 cups chili sauce
1 12-ounce jar orange marmalade
1 cup red wine
½ cup vinegar
1 envelope onion soup mix (½ cup)
¼ teaspoon hot pepper sauce

In 3-quart saucepan cook celery, green pepper, and garlic in butter till tender. Add catsup, chili sauce, marmalade, wine, vinegar, soup mix, pepper sauce, and 1½ cups water. Bring to boil; reduce heat. Simmer, uncovered, 15 minutes; stir often. Cool quickly. Pour into half-pint freezer containers; leave 1-inch headspace. Seal, label, and freeze. Makes 8 half-pints.

Directions to pack with sauce: Keep frozen till ready to use. To use: Thaw. Baste meats *or* vegetables with sauce during last 10 minutes of barbecuing. Heat remaining sauce to pass.

Tomato Cocktail Sauce

3 tablespoons sugar
2 tablespoons cornstarch
2½ cups vegetable juice cocktail
1 12-ounce bottle chili sauce
⅓ cup cooking oil
2 tablespoons lemon juice
2 tablespoons prepared
horseradish
1 teaspoon Worcestershire sauce
¼ teaspoon bottled hot pepper
sauce

In saucepan combine sugar, cornstarch, and ¾ teaspoon salt. Slowly blend in vegetable cocktail. Cook and stir till thickened. Stir in next six ingredients. Bring to boiling. Pour into hot, clean half-pint jars; leave ½-inch headspace. Adjust lids. Process in boiling water bath 10 minutes. (Start timing when water returns to boiling.) Makes 4 half-pints.

Directions to pack with sauce: Shake sauce well before using. Serve chilled with meat or seafood *or* blend ¼ to ½ cup of sauce with ½ cup mayonnaise and use as a salad dressing.

Spiced Lemon Vinegar

A tangy vinegar shown on pages 86-87—

1 ⁴/₅-quart bottle dry sherry
2 cups white vinegar
9 inches stick cinnamon
3 8-inch strips lemon peel
10 seedless green grapes

Mix sherry, vinegar, *3 inches stick cinnamon,* and *1 strip lemon peel* in saucepan. Bring to boil; simmer 15 minutes. Strain into two clean pint bottles. To each bottle add 3 inches stick cinnamon, 1 strip lemon peel, and 5 grapes. Seal with caps or corks. Makes 2 pints.

Directions to pack with vinegar: Use with salad oil as a salad dressing.

Tarragon Vinegar

½ to 1 cup fresh tarragon leaves
1 cup white vinegar
1 whole clove
1 small clove garlic

Rinse and dry tarragon; snip lightly. Mix in jar with vinegar, clove, and garlic. Cover; let stand 24 hours at room temperature. Remove garlic. Let vinegar stand, covered, 2 weeks. Strain; pour into an attractive container. Cover tightly. Makes 1 cup.

Homemade Horseradish Mustard

2 vegetable bouillon cubes
4 teaspoons cornstarch
4 teaspoons sugar
4 teaspoons dry mustard
2 teaspoons ground turmeric
¼ cup white wine vinegar
4 teaspoons prepared horseradish
2 slightly beaten egg yolks

Dissolve bouillon in 1½ cups hot water. In saucepan blend cornstarch, sugar, mustard, and turmeric. Stir in vinegar and horseradish. Slowly blend in bouillon. Cook and stir over low heat till thickened and bubbly. Stir a moderate amount into egg yolks. Return to saucepan. Cook and stir 1 minute. Pack in ½-cup containers. Refrigerate. Makes 1½ cups.

Directions to pack with mustard: Store mustard, covered, in refrigerator.

Seasoned Salt

    1 cup pickling salt
    2½ teaspoons paprika
    2 teaspoons dry mustard
    1½ teaspoons dried oregano,
       crushed
    1½ teaspoons garlic powder
    1 teaspoon dried thyme, crushed
    1 teaspoon curry powder
    ½ teaspoon onion powder
    ¼ teaspoon dried dillweed

Combine salt, paprika, mustard, oregano, garlic powder, thyme, curry powder, onion powder, and dillweed. Mix thoroughly. Package in airtight containers. Seal. Makes 1 cup.

Make-Your-Own-Curry

    ¼ cup coriander seed
    ¼ cup ground turmeric
    4 inches stick cinnamon, broken
    1 tablespoon cumin seed
    1 tablespoon cardamom pods,
       shelled (about 1 teaspoon
       seed)
    1 teaspoon whole black pepper
    1 teaspoon ground ginger
    5 whole cloves
    2 bay leaves

Place all ingredients in shallow baking pan. Bake at 200° for 25 minutes, stirring occasionally. Place mixture in blender container. Cover; blend till well ground. Package in ¼-cup portions. Makes ¾ cup.

Poultry Seasoning

    2 cups dried parsley
    1 cup rubbed sage
    ½ cup dried rosemary, crushed
    ½ cup dried marjoram, crushed
    3 tablespoons salt
    1 tablespoon pepper
    2 teaspoons onion powder
    ½ teaspoon ground ginger

Combine parsley, sage, rosemary, marjoram, salt, pepper, onion powder, and ginger. Pour into air-tight containers. Seal. Before using shake mixture well. Makes 4 cups.

Homemade Granola Mix

    2½ cups regular rolled oats
    1 cup shredded coconut
    ½ cup coarsely chopped almonds
    ½ cup sesame seeds
    ½ cup shelled sunflower seeds
    ½ cup wheat germ
    ½ cup honey
    ¼ cup cooking oil
    ½ cup snipped dried apricots
    ½ cup raisins

In bowl combine oats, coconut, almonds, sesame seeds, sunflower seeds, and wheat germ. Combine honey and oil. Stir into oat mixture. Spread out in 13x9x2-inch baking pan. Bake at 300° till light brown, 45 to 50 minutes; stir every 15 minutes. Remove from oven; stir in apricots and raisins. Remove to another pan. Cool; stir often to prevent lumping. Pack in tightly covered jars or plastic bags. Makes 6½ cups.

Directions to pack with mix: To store more than two weeks, seal in plastic bags and freeze.

Camper's Pancake Mix

    12 cups all-purpose flour
    4 cups nonfat dry milk powder
    ¾ cup baking powder
    ¾ cup sugar
    2 tablespoons salt

Stir together flour, nonfat dry milk powder, baking powder, sugar, and salt thoroughly. Package in tightly covered container. Makes about 17½ cups mix.

Directions to pack with mix: Use mix to make the following recipe:

Camper's Pancakes: In mixing bowl combine 1½ cups **Camper's Pancake Mix,** 1 cup **water, 1 egg,** and 2 tablespoons **cooking oil.** Beat smooth with rotary beater. Using ¼-cup batter for each pancake, bake on hot lightly greased griddle, turning once, Makes 8.

Give two gifts in one with *Homemade Granola Mix.* ▶
This combination of oats, coconut, honey, and dried apricots can be eaten alone or with milk as a snack or breakfast cereal, or it can be used to make recipes such as *Granola Ripple Cake* (see recipe, page 24).

Party-Going Snacks

Soft Whole Wheat Pretzels

If you enjoy chewy foods, these pretzels, shown on pages 52-53, are for you—

> 3 cups all-purpose flour
> 1½ tablespoons sesame seed, toasted
> 1 package active dry yeast
> 2½ cups milk
> ½ cup sugar
> ¼ cup cooking oil
> 1½ teaspoons salt
> 3 cups whole wheat flour
>
> ● ● ●
>
> 3 tablespoons salt
> 8 cups boiling water
> 1 slightly beaten egg white
> Coarse salt *or* sesame seed, toasted

In mixing bowl combine *2 cups* of the all-purpose flour, the 1½ tablespoons sesame seed, and yeast. In saucepan heat milk, sugar, cooking oil, and 1½ teaspoons salt just till warm (115 to 120°). Add to dry mixture. Beat at low speed of electric mixer for ½ minute, scraping sides of bowl constantly. Beat 3 minutes at high speed. By hand, stir in whole wheat flour and enough remaining all-purpose flour to make a moderately stiff dough. Knead on floured surface till smooth, about 5 minutes. Shape into a ball. Place in greased bowl, turning once. Cover; let rise till double (about 50 minutes). Punch down; turn out on floured surface. Cover; let rest 10 minutes.

Roll to a 12-inch square. Cut into 12x½-inch strips. Roll each strip to a rope 16 inches long. Shape into pretzels by forming a knot and looping ends through. Let rise, uncovered, 20 minutes. Dissolve 3 tablespoons salt in boiling water. Lower 1 or 2 pretzels at a time into boiling water. Boil for 1 minute on each side. Remove to paper toweling with slotted spoon. Pat dry. Arrange pretzels ½ inch apart on well-greased baking sheets. Brush with a mixture of egg white and 1 tablespoon water. Sprinkle pretzels lightly with coarse salt or sesame seed. Bake at 350° till golden brown, about 25 minutes. Makes 24.

Spicy Sherried Walnuts

Mix nuts and wine for this snack shown on page 55—

In saucepan blend 1½ cups packed **brown sugar,** ¼ cup **sherry,** 2 tablespoons **corn syrup,** 1 teaspoon **pumpkin pie spice,** and ¼ teaspoon **salt.** Heat till sugar is dissolved. Stir in 5 cups **walnut halves** till well coated. Roll in **granulated sugar.** Dry on baking sheets. Store in a loosely covered container. Makes 5 cups.

Peppy Almonds

> 2 tablespoons butter *or* margarine, melted
> 1 teaspoon salt
> 1 teaspoon celery salt
> 1 teaspoon chili powder
> ⅛ teaspoon cayenne
> 1½ cups whole shelled almonds

In baking pan mix butter, salt, celery salt, chili powder, and cayenne. Stir in almonds. Bake at 375° for 15 minutes, stirring occasionally. Makes 1½ cups.

Corn-Nut Snack

Bring this irresistible snack, shown on pages 52-53, to the next party you attend—

> ¼ cup butter *or* margarine
> 1 tablespoon curry powder
> 2 teaspoons onion salt
> ½ teaspoon ground ginger
> 6 cups bite-size shredded corn squares
> 2 cups mixed nuts (one 12-ounce can)
> 1 3-ounce can chow mein noodles
> 1 cup raisins

In a 13x9x2-inch baking pan melt butter in a 275° oven. Remove pan from oven. Add curry powder, onion salt, and ginger; mix well. Stir in cereal, nuts, and chow mein noodles till coated. Bake, uncovered, at 275° for 30 minutes. Cool. Add raisins. Makes 11½ cups.

Parmesan Nibble Mix

6 cups round oat cereal
3 cups pretzel sticks
3 cups beer nuts
½ cup butter *or* margarine, melted
1 envelope Parmesan salad
      dressing mix (1 tablespoon)

In 13x9x2-inch baking pan heat oat cereal in a 300° oven till warm, about 5 minutes. Remove from oven. Add pretzels and nuts. Pour melted butter *or* margarine over cereal mixture. Sprinkle with dry salad dressing mix. Coat mixture thoroughly. Return to oven and heat 15 to 20 minutes more. Cool. Store in loosely covered container. Makes 12 cups.

Cheddar in Red Wine

Jars of this robust cheese, pictured on pages 86-87, make a unique appetizer for almost any gathering—

Cut 8 ounces sharp **Cheddar cheese** into ½-inch cubes. Pack loosely in a quart jar. Pour 1 cup **Burgundy** over cheese. Cover tightly. Store in refrigerator 3 days. Shake gently several times each day. Pack cheese in smaller decorative jars for giving.
   Directions to pack with cheese: Keep cheese refrigerated. Serve as an appetizer.

Sherry-Cheese Spread

Serve this elegant cheese and wine combination, shown on pages 86-87, at room temperature—

4 cups shredded Cheddar cheese
      (16 ounces)
½ cup crumbled blue cheese
      (2 ounces)
½ cup dry sherry
¼ cup butter, softened
2 teaspoons dry mustard
   Dash cayenne

In mixing bowl combine Cheddar, blue cheese, sherry, butter, mustard, and cayenne. Beat with electric mixer till well blended. Pack into lightly oiled 1-cup molds or containers. Cover tightly. Refrigerate. Makes 4 cups.
   Directions to pack with spread: Keep refrigerated. Let stand at room temperature before serving. Serve with crackers.

Cheesy Bacon Spread

4 cups shredded Swiss cheese
      (16 ounces)
2 4-ounce containers Neufchatel
      cheese spread with bacon and
      horseradish
1 cup shredded Gruyere cheese
      (4 ounces)
½ cup milk
¼ cup snipped parsley

Bring Swiss cheese, Neufchatel cheese spread, and Gruyere to room temperature. In mixing bowl combine cheeses. Beat with electric mixer till cheese mixture is fluffy. Blend in milk. Stir in snipped parsley. Pack in four 1-cup containers (*or* form into four cheese balls and roll in chopped walnuts, if desired). Refrigerate till firm. Makes 4 cups.
   Directions to pack with spread: Keep refrigerated till ready to use. Before serving unmold; sprinkle with paprika. Serve with crackers.

For a unique hostess gift, try giving *Parmesan Nibble Mix* in a sea chest made from a shoe box or in tall glasses decorated as pirates.

Double Cheese and Beef Log

2 cups shredded sharp Cheddar
  cheese (8 ounces)
1 3-ounce package cream cheese
  with chives
• • •
¼ cup dry white wine
1 teaspoon prepared horseradish
½ cup snipped smoked beef

Let Cheddar and cream cheese stand at room temperature for 1 hour. In mixing bowl combine Cheddar and cream cheese, wine, and horseradish. Beat with electric mixer till well blended. Cover; chill 1 hour. Shape cheese mixture into a log about 1½ inches in diameter. Roll log in chopped beef. Wrap in clear plastic wrap. Refrigerate. Makes 1¾ cups.

Directions to pack with log: Keep refrigerated. Serve with assorted crackers.

Four Cheese Ball

1 cup shredded Swiss cheese
  (4 ounces)
1 cup shredded American cheese
  (4 ounces)
1 3-ounce package cream cheese,
  softened
¼ cup mayonnaise *or* salad
  dressing
2 tablespoons chopped pimiento
1 teaspoon Worcestershire
  sauce
½ teaspoon onion powder
¼ teaspoon bottled hot pepper
  sauce
½ cup crushed potato chips
1½ teaspoons grated Parmesan
  cheese

Bring Swiss cheese and American cheese to room temperature. In small mixing bowl beat together cream cheese and mayonnaise with electric mixer. Beat in Swiss and American cheeses. Add pimiento, Worcestershire, onion powder, and pepper sauce. Chill at least 1 hour. Shape into a ball. Mix potato chips and Parmesan. Press over outside of ball. Wrap in clear plastic wrap. Refrigerate till firm. Makes 1 ball.

Directions to pack with ball: Keep refrigerated. Serve with assorted crackers.

Braunschweiger Dip

1 pound braunschweiger
2 8-ounce cartons onion sour
  cream dip (2 cups)
½ cup finely chopped dill pickle
2 tablespoons milk
1 tablespoon prepared mustard
¼ teaspoon bottled hot pepper
  sauce

Beat all ingredients together with electric mixer till blended. Pack in four 1-cup containers. Cover; refrigerate. Makes 4 cups.

Directions to pack with dip: Keep refrigerated. Serve with vegetable dippers.

Party Tuna Ball

4 3-ounce packages cream cheese
  with chives, softened
2 tablespoons lemon juice
2 teaspoons Worcestershire sauce
¼ teaspoon onion powder
  Several dashes bottled hot
  pepper sauce
2 6½- *or* 7-ounce cans tuna,
  drained and finely flaked
½ cup finely chopped celery
¾ cup chopped walnuts
½ cup snipped parsley

Blend first five ingredients. Stir in tuna and celery; mix well. Chill several hours. On waxed paper combine nuts and parsley. Shape tuna mixture into three balls. Roll each ball in nut mixture. Wrap in clear plastic wrap. Refrigerate. Makes 3 balls.

Directions to pack with balls: Store in refrigerator. Serve with assorted crackers.

Seafood-Cheese Dip

Beat together two 8-ounce packages **cream cheese,** softened; ¼ cup **dry sherry;** 3 tablespoons **milk;** and ½ teaspoon prepared **horseradish.** Fold in two 4½-ounce cans **shrimp,** drained and finely chopped and ¼ cup chopped **green onions** with tops. Pack into 3 or 4 containers. Cover; refrigerate. Makes 3½ cups.

Directions to pack with dip: Keep refrigerated. Serve with vegetable dippers.

Gift-Worthy Beverages

Café au Lait Mix

Combine one 6-ounce jar instant **non-dairy creamer** (1½ cups), ¼ cup packed **brown sugar,** ¼ cup instant **coffee crystals,** and dash **salt.** Store in airtight containers. Makes 2 cups.

Directions to pack with mix: For one serving, mix ¼ cup mix with ⅔ cup boiling water in cup.

Orange Jupiter Mix

  1¾ cups nonfat dry milk powder
  1 9-ounce jar orange-flavored
      breakfast drink powder
      (1¼ cups)
  ½ cup sugar
  2 teaspoons vanilla

Stir together milk powder, breakfast drink powder, and sugar. Blend in vanilla. Store in airtight containers. Makes about 4 cups mix.

Directions to pack with mix: For *three servings:* In blender container place 1 cup mix and 1½ cups cold water. Cover; blend till smooth. Add 5 or 6 ice cubes, 1 cube at a time, blending till chopped after each addition.

For one serving: In blender container place ⅓ cup mix, ½ cup cold water, and 2 ice cubes. Cover; blend till smooth, 30 to 45 seconds.

Minty Chocolate Malt Mix

  2 cups chocolate-flavored malted
      milk powder
  ½ cup white butter mints, chopped
  3 cups nonfat dry milk powder
  ½ cup sweetened cocoa mix

In blender container mix *1 cup* malted milk powder and mints. Blend till mints are finely chopped, about 1 minute. Turn into mixing bowl. Add remaining malted milk powder, nonfat dry milk powder, and cocoa mix. Stir well. Store in airtight containers. Makes 5¾ cups.

Directions to pack with mix: For one serving, mix ¼ cup mix with ¾ cup boiling water in a cup. Stir to dissolve mixture.

Hot Chocolate Mix

  1 8-quart package nonfat dry
      milk powder
  1 16-ounce can sweetened cocoa
      mix
  1 pound sifted powdered sugar
  1 6-ounce jar powdered non-dairy
      creamer

Combine dry milk powder, cocoa mix, powdered sugar, and non-dairy creamer. Mix thoroughly. Store in airtight containers. Makes 15 cups mix.

Directions to pack with mix: For one serving, combine ¼ cup mix with ¾ cup boiling water in a cup or mug. Stir to dissolve mixture. Top with marshmallow, if desired.

Spiced Mocha Mix

  2 cups sweetened cocoa mix
  ⅓ cup instant coffee crystals
  1 teaspoon ground cinnamon

Combine cocoa mix, coffee crystals, and cinnamon. Stir thoroughly. Store in airtight containers. Makes 2¼ cups mix.

Directions to pack with mix: For one serving, combine 3 tablespoons mix with ⅔ cup boiling water in a cup or mug.

Hot Tea Mix

  1 9-ounce jar orange-flavored
      breakfast drink powder
      (1¼ cups)
  ¾ cup iced tea mix with lemon
      and sugar
  1 teaspoon ground cinnamon
  ½ teaspoon ground allspice
  ¼ teaspoon ground cloves

Combine all ingredients; mix well. Store in airtight containers. Makes 2 cups mix.

Directions to pack with mix: For one serving, combine 2 tablespoons mix with 1 cup boiling water in a cup or mug.

Blackberry Brandy

4 cups fresh blackberries
2 cups brandy
¾ cup sugar
¾ teaspoon whole allspice
12 whole cloves

Wash fruit; drain. In gallon screw-top jar mix fruit and remaining ingredients. Cover tightly. Invert jar; let stand 24 hours. Turn jar upright; let stand 24 hours. Repeat turning process till sugar is dissolved. Store in cool, dark place at least 2 months. Strain through cheesecloth into a decanter. Cover. Makes 3½ cups.

Plum Cordial

3 pounds fresh purple plums,
   halved and pitted (7 cups)
4 cups sugar
4 cups gin

In gallon screw-top jar mix all ingredients. Cover tightly. Invert jar; let stand 24 hours. Turn jar upright; let stand 24 hours. Repeat turning till sugar dissolves. Store in cool, dark place 2 months. Strain through cheesecloth into decanters. Cover. Makes 8 cups.

Apple Cordial

4 cups coarsely chopped apple
2 cups brandy
1 cup sugar
4 inches stick cinnamon, broken

In large screw-top jar combine all ingredients. Cover tightly. Invert jar; let stand 24 hours. Turn jar upright; let stand 24 hours. Repeat turning process till sugar dissolves. Store in cool, dark place 4 to 6 weeks. Strain through cheesecloth into decanter. Cover. Makes 2½ cups.

◀ **Think ahead when giving homemade liqueurs,** as most cordials need three to eight weeks to age. Make your liqueurs when the fruits you need are in season. May through August is the time to make *Blackberry Brandy* (in large decanter and glass) and *Plum Cordial* (in round decanter), while fall is best for *Apple Cordial* (in cordial glass).

Peach Cordial

Sip this golden liqueur shown on pages 52-53 —

3 pounds fresh peaches, pitted
   and quartered
4 cups bourbon
2½ cups sugar
4 strips lemon peel, each 2
   inches long
4 inches stick cinnamon, broken
6 whole cloves

In gallon screw-top jar mix all ingredients. Cover tightly. Invert jar; let stand 24 hours. Turn jar upright; let stand 24 hours. Repeat turning till sugar dissolves. Store in cool, dark place at least 2 months. Strain through cheesecloth into decanters. Cover. Makes 6 cups.

Orange Liqueur

4 medium oranges
2 cups sugar
2 cups vodka *or* rum

Squeeze juice from oranges; reserve peel from *one* orange. Scrape white membrane from reserved peel; cut peel into strips. Add water to juice to make 2 cups. Bring orange juice mixture, peel, and sugar to boiling. Reduce heat; simmer over low heat, 5 minutes. Cool. Pour into large screw-top jar. Stir in vodka. Cover. Let stand at room temperature 3 to 4 weeks. Strain into decanters. Cover. Makes 5 cups.

Cranberry Cordial

Jars of this flavorful cordial and fruit are shown on pages 86-87 —

Wash 4 cups fresh **cranberries;** drain and coarsely chop. Place in large screw-top jar. Add 3 cups **sugar** and 2 cups **gin.** Cover tightly. Invert jar; let stand 24 hours. Turn jar upright; let stand 24 hours. Repeat turning for 3 weeks. Strain through cheesecloth into decanter; cover. Spoon drained berries into a jar. Cover; refrigerate. Give both cordial and cranberries as a gift. Makes 3¼ cups cordial and 3 cups berries.
   Directions to pack with cordial: Serve at room temperature.
   Directions to pack with cranberries: Keep refrigerated. Serve over ice cream.

Gift Bazaar

Need new ideas for a fund-raising sale or a group dinner? Then check the Gift Bazaar.

Here you will discover food gift ideas for donating to a group cause. You'll find cookies, breads, and cakes that will be solid money-earners at a bake sale. You'll also be tempted by casseroles, vegetables, and salads that are ideal for potluck suppers, reunions, or neighbors in need.

When it's crafts you're seeking, try making greeting cards from cookie dough, baskets and ornaments from baker's clay, centerpieces from marzipan, and decorations or party favors from molded sugar.

When you need a gift idea for a special holiday, make one of these. For Easter, Christmas, and weddings choose *Sugar-Molded Decorations* (shown counterclockwise from extreme left) including bells, egg halves, round ornaments, and round or egg-shaped dioramas. At Christmas make *Baker's Clay Ornaments* (beige ornaments at lower right) and *Marzipan Wreath* (center). For St. Valentine's Day, Easter, and Christmas create *Card and Ornament Cookies* (lower left, lower center, and extreme right). (See Index for pages.)

Gifts to Donate

Scotch Teas

The recipes on these two pages are shown on page 76–

1 cup butter *or* margarine,
   melted
2 cups packed brown sugar
2 teaspoons baking powder
½ teaspoon salt
4 cups quick-cooking rolled
   oats

In a medium saucepan combine butter *or* margarine and sugar. Cook and stir till sugar is blended. Stir in baking powder and salt. Add oats and mix thoroughly. Pour into a greased 13x9x2-inch baking pan. Bake at 350°, 20 to 25 minutes. Cool; cut into bars. Makes 4 dozen.

Pumpkin Cookies

2 cups shortening
2 cups sugar
1 16-ounce can pumpkin
2 eggs
2 teaspoons vanilla
4 cups all-purpose flour
2 teaspoons baking powder
2 teaspoons ground cinnamon
1 teaspoon baking soda
1 teaspoon salt
1 teaspoon ground nutmeg
½ teaspoon ground allspice
   ● ● ●
2 cups raisins
1 cup chopped nuts

In mixing bowl thoroughly cream together shortening and sugar. Add pumpkin, eggs, and vanilla. Beat well. Stir together flour, baking powder, cinnamon, baking soda, salt, nutmeg, and allspice. Add to creamed mixture, mixing well. Stir in raisins and nuts. Drop dough from a rounded teaspoon onto a greased cookie sheet, about 2 inches apart. Bake at 350°, 12 to 15 minutes. Remove from baking sheet. Cool. Frost cookies, if desired. Makes 7 dozen.

Gumdrop Gems

1 cup butter *or* margarine
1½ cups sifted powdered sugar
1 teaspoon vanilla
1 egg
2½ cups all-purpose flour
1 teaspoon baking soda
1 teaspoon cream of tartar
¼ teaspoon salt
1 cup small gumdrops, sliced

In mixing bowl cream butter, sugar, and vanilla together well; beat in egg. Stir together flour, soda, cream of tartar, and salt. Stir into creamed mixture till blended. On waxed paper shape dough into 12x2-inch roll. Wrap in waxed paper. Chill several hours *or* overnight. Cut in ¼-inch slices. Keep unsliced portion of roll chilled till needed. Place slices on ungreased cookie sheet, top with gumdrop slices. Bake at 375°, 12 minutes. Cool slightly; remove from sheet. Makes 4 dozen.

Maple Praline Cookies

⅔ cup shortening
⅔ cup packed brown sugar
1 egg
⅓ cup milk
½ teaspoon maple flavoring
2 cups all-purpose flour
¼ teaspoon salt
¼ teaspoon baking soda
2 cups crisp rice cereal
   Granulated sugar
   Pecan halves

In mixing bowl cream shortening and brown sugar till light. Beat in egg. Stir in milk and maple flavoring. (Mixture will look curdled.) Stir together flour, salt, and baking soda. Add to sugar mixture. Mix well. Stir in cereal. Drop dough from teaspoon onto greased cookie sheet, about 2 inches apart. Flatten cookies with bottom of glass dipped in granulated sugar. Top each with pecan half. Bake at 375°, 8 to 10 minutes. Makes 4 dozen.

Nut-Edged Butter Slices

½ cup butter *or* margarine
⅔ cup sugar
1 egg yolk
2 tablespoons milk
1 teaspoon vanilla
1½ cups all-purpose flour
2 teaspoons baking powder
½ teaspoon salt

• • •

½ cup finely chopped almonds,
   toasted
3 tablespoons sugar
1 slightly beaten egg white

In mixing bowl cream butter *or* margarine and ⅔ cup sugar together thoroughly. Add egg yolk, milk, and vanilla; beat well. Stir together flour, baking powder, and salt. Gradually add to creamed mixture, beating well. Shape dough on waxed paper into a 12x1½-inch roll. Wrap in waxed paper. Chill 1 hour. Combine nuts and the 3 tablespoons sugar. Brush chilled dough with egg white and roll in almond mixture, pressing nuts in firmly. Cut in ¼-inch slices. Place on lightly greased cookie sheet; bake at 400° till golden brown, 7 to 10 minutes. Makes 4 dozen cookies.

Apple-Orange Brownies

⅔ cup butter *or* margarine
2 cups packed brown sugar
1 8-ounce can applesauce
2 eggs
1 tablespoon grated orange
   peel
2 teaspoons vanilla
2 cups all-purpose flour
2 teaspoons baking powder
1 teaspoon salt
½ teaspoon baking soda
1 cup chopped walnuts

In saucepan melt butter *or* margarine; remove from heat. Add brown sugar. Stir till sugar is blended. Cool. Beat in applesauce, eggs, orange peel, and vanilla. Stir together flour, baking powder, salt, and baking soda. Stir into applesauce mixture. Stir in nuts. Spread in greased 15½x10½x1-inch jelly roll pan. Bake at 350°, 25 to 30 minutes. Makes 4 dozen.

Prune Bars

½ of 6-ounce can frozen lemonade
   concentrate, thawed (6
   tablespoons)
1 cup snipped, pitted prunes
   (6 ounces)
½ cup packed brown sugar
⅓ cup chopped walnuts
2 tablespoons all-purpose flour
⅛ teaspoon salt

• • •

1 cup all-purpose flour
1 cup quick-cooking rolled oats
½ cup packed brown sugar
½ teaspoon ground cinnamon
½ cup butter *or* margarine

Add enough water to lemonade concentrate to make 1 cup liquid. In saucepan simmer prunes in lemonade mixture, covered, till tender, 4 to 5 minutes. Mix ½ cup brown sugar, walnuts, 2 tablespoons flour, and salt; add to prune mixture. Cook and stir till very thick, about 5 minutes. Cool thoroughly.

Mix 1 cup flour, oats, ½ cup brown sugar, and cinnamon. Cut in butter *or* margarine till mixture is crumbly; mix well. Pat *half* of the oat mixture in a greased 9x9x2-inch baking pan. Spread with cooled prune filling. Crumble remaining oat mixture over top; press lightly into filling. Bake at 350° for 30 to 35 minutes. Cool; cut into bars. Makes 24.

Easy Toffee

½ cup butter *or* margarine,
   melted
¾ cup packed brown sugar
½ cup semisweet chocolate pieces

• • •

1 cup chopped walnuts

In a 1½-quart saucepan combine butter *or* margarine and brown sugar. Cook over medium heat to soft-crack stage *or* till candy thermometer registers 290°, stirring often. Remove from heat and spread into a buttered 8x8x2-inch baking pan. Sprinkle chocolate pieces atop. Let stand 1 to 2 minutes. When chocolate is softened, spread evenly over toffee and sprinkle wanuts atop. Chill thoroughly; break into pieces. Makes about 1 pound.

Quick Banana Bread

   4 cups packaged biscuit mix
   1 cup sugar
   ½ cup all-purpose flour
   ½ teaspoon baking soda
   4 beaten eggs
   1 cup dairy sour cream
   2 cups mashed ripe banana
        (4 medium)
   1 cup chopped walnuts

In large mixing bowl combine biscuit mix, sugar, flour, and baking soda. Combine eggs and sour cream; stir into dry ingredients with mashed banana. Stir in chopped walnuts. Pour into two greased 9x5x3-inch loaf pans. Bake at 350° till bread tests done, about 50 minutes. Cool 10 minutes in pans; remove from pans. Cool on rack. Makes 2 loaves.

Grandma's Fruit Bread

In small bowl cover 1 cup snipped dried **apricots** with warm **water;** let stand 5 minutes. Drain well; set aside. In mixing bowl cream together thoroughly ½ cup **shortening** and 1½ cups **sugar.** Add 4 **eggs;** beat till light. Stir together 4 cups all-purpose **flour,** 2 tablespoons **baking powder,** and 1 teaspoon **salt.** Add dry ingredients to creamed mixture alternately with 2 cups **milk,** beating well after each addition. Stir in reserved apricots, 1 cup snipped pitted **prunes,** and ½ cup chopped **walnuts.** Pour batter into two greased and floured 9x5x3-inch loaf pans. Bake at 350° till loaves test done, 60 to 65 minutes. Cool 10 minutes in pans. Remove from pans; cool loaves on rack. Wrap and store loaves overnight before slicing. Makes 2 loaves.

Need ideas for your next money-raising bake sale? Try (from left to right in top row) *Prune Bars, Maple Praline Cookies, Quick Banana Bread,* (in second row) *Apple-Orange Brownies, Molasses-* *Oat Bread, Pumpkin Cookies, Gumdrop Gems,* (in bottom row) *Grandma's Fruit Bread, Easy Toffee, Scotch Teas, Strawberry Nut Bread,* and *Nut-Edged Butter Slices* (see Index for recipe pages).

Molasses-Oat Bread

In large mixing bowl combine 3 cups all-purpose **flour,** 2 cups **quick-cooking rolled oats,** ¼ cup packed **brown sugar,** 2 packages **active dry yeast,** and 2 teaspoons **salt.** In saucepan mix 1 cup **milk,** ½ cup **water,** ½ cup **shortening,** and ¼ cup light **molasses.** Heat till warm (115 to 120°), stirring constantly. Add molasses mixture with 2 **eggs** to flour mixture. Beat at low speed of electric mixer for ½ minute, scraping sides of bowl. Beat 3 minutes at high speed. By hand, stir in 1¾ to 2 cups all-purpose **flour** to make a soft dough. Turn out on floured surface. Knead till smooth, 4 to 5 minutes. Place in greased bowl; turn once. Cover; let rise till double (1½ hours). Punch down; turn out on floured surface. Divide in half. Shape each half into a loaf. Brush with **water.** Roll in additional **rolled oats.** Place in two greased 8½x4½x2½-inch loaf pans. Cover; let rise till double. Bake at 350°, 40 to 45 minutes. Makes 2.

Strawberry Nut Bread

   1 cup butter *or* margarine
1½ cups sugar
   1 teaspoon vanilla
   ¼ teaspoon lemon extract
   4 eggs
   3 cups all-purpose flour
   1 teaspoon salt
   1 teaspoon cream of tartar
   ½ teaspoon baking soda
   1 cup strawberry jam
   ½ cup dairy sour cream
   1 cup broken walnuts

In mixing bowl cream butter *or* margarine, sugar, vanilla, and lemon extract till fluffy. Add eggs, one at a time, beating well after each addition. Stir together thoroughly flour, salt, cream of tartar, and baking soda. Combine strawberry jam and sour cream. Add jam mixture alternately with dry ingredients to creamed mixture beating till well combined. Stir in walnuts. Divide batter among five greased and floured 4½x2½x1½-inch loaf pans. Bake at 350° till done, 50 to 55 minutes. Cool 10 minutes in pans; remove from pans. Cool on racks. Makes 5 loaves.

Black Walnut Cake

   1 cup butter *or* margarine
   2 cups sifted powdered sugar
   1 teaspoon vanilla
   4 egg yolks
   3 cups sifted cake flour
   1 tablespoon baking powder
   ⅛ teaspoon salt
1⅓ cups milk
   1 cup chopped black walnuts
   4 egg whites
   Sifted powdered sugar

In mixing bowl beat together butter *or* margarine, 2 cups sugar, and vanilla till light and fluffy. Add egg yolks, one at a time, beating well after each addition. Sift together flour, baking powder, and salt. Add alternately to creamed mixture with milk, beating well after each addition. Stir in walnuts. Beat egg whites till stiff peaks form; fold into batter. Pour into a greased and floured 10-inch tube pan. Bake at 350° till cake tests done, about 1 hour. Cool in pan 10 minutes. Remove from pan; cool on rack. When cool dust with additional powdered sugar.

Buttermilk Doughnuts

   ½ cup sugar
   2 slightly beaten eggs
   2 tablespoons butter, melted
3¼ cups all-purpose flour
   1 teaspoon baking soda
   ½ teaspoon baking powder
   ½ teaspoon ground nutmeg
   ⅛ teaspoon salt
   1 cup buttermilk
   Fat for frying

In mixing bowl beat sugar and eggs till light, using electric mixer. Add butter. Stir together flour, baking soda, baking powder, nutmeg, and salt. Add to egg mixture alternately with buttermilk; beat just till blended after each addition. Cover; chill dough 2 hours. Roll dough ½ inch thick on floured surface; cut with 2½-inch doughnut cutter. Fry in deep hot fat (375°) till golden brown, turning once (about 1 minute per side). Drain on paper toweling. While warm sprinkle with additional sugar, if desired. Makes 1½ dozen.

Creamy Potato Salad

9 medium potatoes, cooked, peeled,
and sliced (9 cups)
1 cup chopped celery
⅓ cup sliced green onion with
tops
¼ cup pickle relish
1½ teaspoons salt
⅛ teaspoon pepper
Cream Dressing
½ cup sliced radishes
2 hard-cooked eggs, cut in
wedges

In large bowl combine potatoes, celery, green onion, relish, salt, and pepper. Stir in Cream Dressing. Toss lightly. Chill thoroughly. Before serving, fold in radishes. Garnish with egg wedges. Makes 12 to 16 servings.

Cream Dressing: In saucepan mix 1 tablespoon **sugar**, 2 teaspoons all-purpose **flour**, 1½ teaspoons **dry mustard**; and ¾ teaspoon **salt**. Add 3 slightly beaten **egg yolks** and ¾ cup **milk**. Cook and stir over low heat till thickened *(do not boil)*. Blend in ¼ cup **vinegar** and 3 tablespoons **butter**. Cool. Whip 1 cup **whipping cream** to soft peaks. Fold into cooked mixture.

Tangy Tuna-Macaroni Salad

2½ cups mayonnaise *or* salad
dressing
¼ cup red wine vinegar
1 teaspoon dry mustard
1 teaspoon paprika
¾ teaspoon garlic salt
¼ teaspoon salt
2½ cups cooked shell macaroni
(7 ounces)
2 6½- or 7-ounce cans tuna,
drained and flaked
2 cups chopped celery
⅓ cup sliced pimiento-stuffed
green olives
⅓ cup snipped parsley

In large mixing bowl blend together mayonnaise *or* salad dressing, vinegar, mustard, paprika, garlic salt, and salt. Fold in macaroni, tuna, celery, green olives, and parsley. Cover and chill. Makes 8 to 10 servings.

24-Hour Vegetable Salad

6 cups torn lettuce
Salt
Pepper
Sugar
6 hard-cooked eggs, sliced
1 10-ounce package frozen peas,
thawed (2 cups)
1 pound bacon, crisp-cooked,
drained, and crumbled (1½ cups)
2 cups shredded Swiss cheese
(8 ounces)
1 cup mayonnaise *or* salad
dressing
• • •
¼ cup sliced green onion with
tops
Paprika

In bottom of large bowl place *3 cups* of the lettuce. Sprinkle with salt, pepper, and sugar. Layer egg slices atop lettuce in bowl. Sprinkle with more salt. Layer in order: peas, remaining lettuce, bacon, and Swiss cheese. Spread mayonnaise *or* salad dressing over top, sealing to edge of bowl. Cover and chill 24 hours. Garnish with green onion and paprika. Toss before serving. Makes 12 to 15 servings.

Harvest Fruit Mold

1 12-ounce package mixed dried
fruits
¼ cup sugar
2 3-ounce packages orange-
flavored gelatin
2 cups boiling water
½ cup dry sherry
Leaf lettuce

In saucepan combine dried fruit and enough water to cover the fruit. Simmer gently, covered, 25 to 30 minutes. Add sugar during last 5 minutes of cooking time. Drain fruit, reserving syrup. Add water to syrup to make 1½ cups. Dissolve gelatin in boiling water. Stir in reserved syrup mixture and sherry. Chill till partially set.

Pit prunes; cut up all cooked fruit. Fold into gelatin mixture. Pour into 6-cup ring mold. Chill till firm, 8 hours *or* overnight. Unmold on lettuce. Makes 8 to 10 servings.

Lemon Waldorf Salad

2 3-ounce packages lemon-
   flavored gelatin
2 cups boiling water
1 cup cold water
1 18-ounce can vanilla pudding
    ●   ●   ●
2 cups chopped apple
½ cup chopped celery
½ cup chopped walnuts

Dissolve gelatin in boiling water. Stir in cold water. Chill till partially set. In mixing bowl mix chilled gelatin and pudding. Beat 2 minutes at medium speed of electric mixer. Chill till mixture mounds. Fold in apple, celery, and walnuts. Pour into 7 *or* 8-cup mold. Chill till firm, 6 hours *or* overnight. Makes 10 to 12 servings.

Oven Barbecued Beans

2 pounds dry navy beans
   (5 cups)
10 cups water
1 teaspoon salt
    ●   ●   ●
2 15-ounce cans tomato sauce
2 cups chopped onion
1 cup chopped green pepper
½ cup packed brown sugar
¼ cup vinegar
2 tablespoons Worcestershire
   sauce
2 tablespoons prepared mustard
¼ teaspoon bottled hot pepper
   sauce

Rinse beans. In large saucepan *or* Dutch oven mix beans and water; soak overnight. (Or, bring beans and water to boiling; boil 2 minutes. Remove from heat. Cover; let stand 1 hour.) Do not drain. Add salt to beans. Bring to boiling. Reduce heat; simmer, covered, till tender, 1 to 1¼ hours. Drain the beans well; reserve 2 cups bean liquid.

   In large bean pot mix beans, *1 cup* of reserved liquid, tomato sauce, onion, green pepper, brown sugar, vinegar, Worcestershire, mustard, and pepper sauce. Cover; bake at 300° for 3½ hours. Stir beans occasionally. If necessary, stir in a little of remaining 1 cup reserved bean liquid. Makes 12 to 16 servings.

Bacon-Tomato Rice

4 slices bacon
1 cup chopped onion
½ cup chopped green pepper
2 28-ounce cans tomatoes, cut up
1½ cups regular rice
2 1½-ounce envelopes spaghetti
   sauce mix
1 tablespoon sugar
½ teaspoon salt
½ teaspoon Worcestershire
   sauce
½ cup sliced pitted ripe olives

Cook bacon till crisp. Drain; reserve drippings. Crumble bacon; set aside. Cook onion and pepper in reserved drippings till tender. Add undrained tomatoes, rice, spaghetti sauce mix, sugar, salt, Worcestershire, and 1½ cups water. Simmer, covered, 10 minutes, stirring frequently. Stir in olives. Pour into 2½ *or* 3-quart casserole. Cover. Bake at 350° till rice is done, about 25 minutes. Sprinkle with bacon. Serves 18.

Crowd-Pleasing Vegetable Bake

1 20-ounce package frozen
   cauliflower
1 10-ounce package frozen cut
   broccoli
1 17-ounce can cream-style corn
1 16-ounce can whole kernel corn,
   drained
2 cups shredded Swiss cheese
   (8 ounces)
1 10¾-ounce can condensed cream
   of celery soup
1 3-ounce can sliced mushrooms,
   drained
1½ cups soft rye bread crumbs
   (2 slices)
2 tablespoons butter, melted

Cook cauliflower and broccoli according to package directions. Drain; cut any large pieces of cauliflower in half. Combine corn, cheese, and soup. Fold in cooked vegetables and mushrooms. Turn into 13x9x2-inch baking dish. Mix bread crumbs and butter. Sprinkle atop vegetable mixture. Bake at 375°, 30 to 35 minutes. Let stand 10 minutes before serving. Makes 10 to 12 servings.

Sweet Potato Casserole

  8 medium sweet potatoes
  ⅓ cup raisins
    Salt
  ¾ cup packed brown sugar
  1 tablespoon cornstarch
  ½ teaspoon salt
  ½ teaspoon shredded orange peel
  1 cup orange juice
  ¼ cup butter *or* margarine
  ¼ cup chopped walnuts

Cook potatoes, covered, in large amount boiling salted water just till tender; drain. Peel and slice. Arrange potatoes in 13x9x2-inch baking dish. Sprinkle with raisins. Season with salt. In saucepan combine brown sugar, cornstarch, and ½ teaspoon salt. Blend in orange peel and juice. Cook and stir over medium heat till slightly thickened and bubbly. Cook 1 minute more. Add butter and walnuts, stirring till butter is melted. Pour mixture over potatoes. Bake, uncovered, at 325° till potatoes are well glazed, about 30 minutes. Baste occasionally. Makes 10 to 12 servings.

Going to a potluck dinner? Bring *One-Dish Chicken Supper,* based on chicken noodle soup mix, mushrooms, and cooked chicken.

Turkey Dinner for a Crowd

  1 2-pound boneless turkey roast
    thawed
  8 slices bacon
  1 cup chopped onion
  2 10-ounce packages frozen
    chopped spinach, cooked
    and drained
  3 cups cooked regular rice
  ½ cup sliced celery
  ¼ cup chopped pimiento
  2 10¾-ounce cans condensed cream
    of mushroom soup
  1 cup dairy sour cream
  1½ cups soft bread crumbs
  2 tablespoons butter, melted

Prepare roast according to package directions. Slice into twelve slices. Set aside. Cook bacon till crisp; drain. Reserve ¼ cup drippings. Crumble bacon; set aside. Cook onion in drippings till tender. Mix bacon, onion, spinach, rice, celery, and pimiento. Mix soup and sour cream; stir *half* into rice mixture. Turn into 13x9x2-inch baking dish. Arrange turkey slices atop. Spoon remaining soup mixture over. Mix bread crumbs and butter; sprinkle atop. Bake at 350°, 35 to 40 minutes. Makes 12 servings.

One-Dish Chicken Supper

Drain one 6-ounce can **sliced mushrooms,** reserving liquid. Combine 2 envelopes **chicken-noodle soup mix** and 3 cups **water.** Bring to boiling. Reduce heat. Cover and simmer 5 minutes. Strain to separate broth from noodles; reserve both. Mix reserved broth, mushroom liquid and two 5½-ounce cans **evaporated milk.** In saucepan melt ½ cup **butter** *or* **margarine.** Blend in ½ cup all-purpose **flour,** ½ teaspoon **salt,** and ¼ teaspoon **pepper.** Add broth mixture. Cook and stir till thickened. Break up one 10-ounce package frozen **mixed vegetables** with fork. Add to broth mixture with mushrooms and 4 cups diced cooked **chicken.** Turn into *two* 1½-quart casseroles. Bake, covered, at 350° for 35 minutes. Mix reserved noodles, 4 beaten **eggs,** and ½ teaspoon **salt.** Spoon around edge of casseroles. Bake, covered, 10 minutes more. Makes 12 servings.

Baked Mostaccioli

    8 ounces mostaccioli
    1½ pounds ground beef
    ½ cup chopped onion
    ¼ cup chopped green pepper
    1 clove garlic, minced
    1 28-ounce can tomatoes, cut up
    1 8-ounce can tomato sauce
    1 6-ounce can tomato paste
    1 4-ounce can mushroom stems and
        pieces
    1 teaspoon salt
    1 teaspoon sugar
    1 teaspoon dried basil, crushed
    ⅛ teaspoon pepper
    1 large bay leaf
    ½ cup grated Parmesan cheese
    1 6-ounce package sliced
        mozzarella

Cook mostaccioli in large amount boiling, salted water till *almost* tender, about 7 minutes; drain. Set aside. Meanwhile, in large saucepan cook beef, onion, green pepper, and garlic till meat is browned and vegetables are tender. Drain off fat. Add undrained tomatoes, tomato sauce, tomato paste, undrained mushrooms, salt, sugar, basil, pepper, bay leaf, and ½ cup water. Cover; simmer for 30 minutes. Remove bay leaf. Stir in mostaccioli. Turn into 13x9x2-inch baking dish. Sprinkle with Parmesan cheese. Cover with foil. Bake at 350° for 35 minutes. Remove foil. Place mozzarella slices atop. Bake 5 minutes more. Serves 8 to 10.

Sausage au Gratin

In large bowl blend together two 8-ounce jars **cheese spread** and 2 cups dairy **sour cream.** Stir in 2 tablespoons **instant minced onion,** 1-tablespoon dry **parsley flakes,** and 1 teaspoon **salt.** Fold in 12 medium **potatoes,** cooked, peeled, and sliced along with one 12-ounce package fully-cooked **smoked sausage links,** sliced. Turn into a 13x9x2-inch baking dish. Bake, uncovered, at 350° for 40 to 45 minutes. Mix 1½ cups **soft bread crumbs,** 1 tablespoon melted **butter,** and ¼ teaspoon **paprika.** Sprinkle atop casserole. Bake 10 minutes more. Serves 12.

Ham Potluck Supper

    ½ cup chopped onion
    ½ cup chopped green pepper
    ¼ cup butter
    ⅓ cup all-purpose flour
    2 10½-ounce cans condensed
        chicken with rice soup
    1 cup milk
    3 cups cubed fully cooked ham
    7 hard-cooked eggs, sliced
    1½ cups soft bread crumbs
    2 tablespoons butter, melted

Cook onion and pepper in ¼ cup butter till tender. Stir in flour; add soup. Stir in milk. Cook and stir till thickened. Fold in ham and *six* of the eggs. Turn into 12x7½x2-inch baking dish. Mix bread crumbs and remaining butter. Sprinkle around edge of baking dish. Bake at 350°, 25 minutes. Garnish with remaining egg slices. Makes 10 servings.

Totable Tuna Bake

    1 cup sliced celery
    ½ cup chopped onion
    ¼ cup butter *or* margarine
    2 10¾-ounce cans condensed cream
        of celery soup
    1½ cups shredded American cheese
    1 cup milk
    ½ cup mayonnaise
    8 ounces medium noodles, cooked
    3 6½- or 7-ounce cans tuna,
        drained and coarsely flaked
    1 4-ounce can mushroom stems and
        pieces, drained
    ¼ cup sliced pimiento stuffed
        olives
    2 cups soft bread crumbs
    ¼ cup toasted sliced almonds

In saucepan cook celery and onion in *half* of the butter till tender. Stir in soup, cheese, milk, and mayonnaise; mix well. Fold in noodles, tuna, mushrooms, and olives. Turn into 13x9x2-inch baking dish. Bake, uncovered, at 375° for 20 minutes. Melt remaining butter. Mix with bread crumbs. Sprinkle around edges of baking dish. Arrange almonds in center. Bake till heated through, 10 to 15 minutes more. Serves 10 to 12.

Gifts too Pretty to Eat

Baker's Clay Dough

Use this basic dough for the Lattice Basket, Baker's Clay Ornaments, and Marzipan Wreath–

2½ cups all-purpose flour
1 cup salt
1 cup water

In large mixing bowl combine all-purpose flour, salt, and water. Mix thoroughly with spoon till all the flour is moistened. Turn dough out onto a lightly floured surface. Knead till smooth, about 10 minutes.

Shape into a ball; return to bowl. Keep covered with a damp cloth *or* paper towel till ready to use. Before beginning project, check the consistency of dough. If the dough is too sticky, add a small amount of additional flour. If dough is too stiff, knead in several teaspoons additional water. (This dough is intended for craft projects. Please do not eat it.)

For a *Lattice Basket* weave strips of *Baker's Clay Dough* on an inverted foil-lined baking dish. Keep the strips ½ inch apart. Moisten all areas where dough overlaps and press each seam with the blunt end of a pen or pencil. This insures the weave will hold together during baking.

Lattice Basket

Prepare a double recipe of **Baker's Clay Dough.** Roll dough to a 20x16-inch rectangle on a floured surface. Cut twelve 20x¾-inch strips, two 10x¾-inch strips, and two 6x¾-inch strips. Reserve remaining dough.

Cover a baking sheet with foil. Spray foil with nonstick vegetable coating. Invert a 10x-6x2-inch baking dish on foil-lined baking sheet. Cover bottom and sides of dish with foil. Spray with vegetable coating. Lay five 20-inch strips lengthwise on baking dish, about ½-inch apart. Cut seven 20-inch strips to a length of 12 inches. Weave these strips crosswise through long strips on baking dish to form lattice pattern. Be sure to keep strips about ½ inch apart. (See picture at left.)

Weave the two 10-inch strips along long edges of casserole and the two 6-inch strips along short edges. Dip finger in water and moisten between all of the overlapping woven dough pieces. Use blunt end of pen or pencil to imprint all overlapping areas to help hold them together (see picture at left). Using scissors cut all woven dough strips ½ inch shorter than sides of baking dish.

Roll remaining dough into a 40-inch rope, ½ inch in diameter. Position rope around basket edge, making sure to round corners to fit basket. Dampen one side of rope with water and press firmly into all cut ends of dough around the edge of basket.

Bake basket on baking sheet at 300° for 3 hours. Cool till easily handled. Turn baking dish and basket upright. Carefully remove dish and foil. Replace basket right side up on foil-lined baking sheet and return to oven. Continue baking till inside of basket is firm, 1 to 2 hours more. Cool thoroughly.

Apply several coats of **polyurethane varnish,** drying well between coats. Brush top edge with a thick layer of **white glue.** Sprinkle with **birdseed.** Dry basket thoroughly.

Once you've gained experience, you can vary the basic lattice basket by using round or oval oven-proof baking dishes.

Baker's Clay Ornaments

These ornaments are shown on pages 72-73—

Prepare a single recipe of **Baker's Clay Dough.** Roll dough on floured surface to ⅛- to ¼-inch thickness. Cut with horse, angel, stocking, star, *or* tree-shaped cookie cutters. Use excess dough to add three-dimensional trim to ornaments (see photo, pages 72-73). Make sure to moisten trim pieces before attaching to ornament. Press trim firmly to ornament.

Place ornaments on lightly greased cookie sheets. With a skewer make holes in tops of ornaments for hangers. Brush ornaments with 1 beaten **egg.** Bake at 325° till hard, 25 to 30 minutes. Cool on wire racks. When cool insert pieces of **yarn** *or* **ribbon** in hole at tops of ornaments; tie yarn or ribbon in a loop for hangers. Makes about 2 dozen.

Marzipan Wreath

Use this wreath, on pages 72-73, as a centerpiece—

Cut cardboard patterns for 8-inch and 5¼-inch circles and for 1¼-inch and 2½-inch leaves. Prepare **Baker's Clay Dough.** Roll *half* to 9-inch circle. Use circle patterns to cut out wreath. Place on ungreased baking sheet. Bake at 325°, 35 to 40 minutes. (If wreath buckles, weight down while warm.)

Roll remaining dough ⅛ inch thick. Cut out 24 leaves of each size, using patterns. Draw veins in leaves with wooden pick. Bake on baking sheet at 325°, 25 to 30 minutes.

Cool leaves on racks. Brush wreath and leaves with a mixture of **water** and **green food coloring.** Dry. Tint **Powdered Sugar Frosting** (see recipe, page 84) green. Use frosting as glue, arrange **Marzipan Fruit** (see recipe, page 84) and leaves on wreath. Dry.

Transform *Baker's Clay Dough* into attractive long-lasting gifts. All you need is flour, salt, water, and an ovenproof baking dish. Start with easy projects such as this *Lattice Basket,* then move on to your own version of complicated variations such as the round basket in the background.

Marzipan Fruit

In buttered 1-quart saucepan mix 2 cups **sugar,** 1½ cups **water,** and 2 tablespoons **light corn syrup.** Cook and stir till sugar dissolves and mixture boils. Cook *without stirring* to soft-ball stage *or* till candy thermometer registers 240°. Pour onto large platter. *Do not scrape pan.* Cool about 30 minutes. *Do not move.* With spatula scrape candy from edge of platter toward center till creamy, about 5 minutes. Knead 10 minutes. Store in covered container 24 hours. With hands work in two 8-ounce cans **almond paste.** Divide dough into six portions. Tint two portions red, two portions yellow, one portion green, and one portion purple with **paste fool coloring.** Wrap portions not being used in foil. Shape fruits as directed below. Makes 1½ pounds.

Apples: Using 1½ teaspoons red candy for each, form balls. Add **whole clove** for blossom end. Dry, uncovered, overnight. Brush with **light corn syrup.** Dry overnight.

Strawberries: Using 1 teaspoon red candy for each, form balls. Shape a rounded point at one end; flatten other end. Insert **plastic green leaves** in flattened end. Dry, uncovered, overnight. Brush with **light corn syrup;** roll in **red sugar.** Dry, uncovered, overnight.

Cherries: Using ¼ teaspoon red candy for each, form balls. Use wooden pick to make indentation in center of each cherry. Insert 1-inch piece of **green florist wire.** Dry, uncovered, overnight. Brush with **light corn syrup.** Dry.

Pears: Using 2 teaspoons green *or* yellow candy for each, form pears. Add **whole clove** for blossom end. Dry overnight. Brush with a mixture of **red food coloring** and **water** for blush. Brush with **light corn syrup.** Dry.

Bananas: Shape bananas using 1 teaspoon yellow candy for each. Dry, overnight. Tint ends with mixture of equal parts **cocoa powder** and **water.** Make streaks on fruit. Dry.

Oranges: Work 1 to 2 drops **red food coloring** into remaining yellow candy. Using 1½ teaspoons candy for each, form balls. Roll over vegetable grater for stippling. Dry. Brush with **light corn syrup.** Dry overnight.

Grapes: Using 2 teaspoons purple candy for each cluster, form tiny balls and arrange into clusters.. Dry overnight. Brush with **light corn syrup;** roll in **sugar.** Dry well. Paint dark purple edge on each grape. Dry.

Card and Ornament Cookies

Make cards or ornaments like those on pages 72-73—

Basic Dough: Cream 1½ cups **butter** and 2 cups packed **brown sugar;** add 1 **egg.** Beat till light. Mix 4 cups all-purpose **flour,** 2 teaspoons ground **cinnamon,** 1 teaspoon ground **nutmeg,** ½ teaspoon ground **cloves,** and ¼ teaspoon **baking soda.** Stir into egg mixture. Cover; chill 2 hours.

Valentine and Easter Card Cookies: Cut heart-shaped *or* egg-shaped pattern 5 inches long from paper. For each cookie roll ⅓ cup **Basic Dough** to ¼-inch thickness directly on ungreased cookie sheet. Cut into heart *or* egg shape, using pattern. Remove excess dough. Bake 2 or 3 cookies on each sheet. Bake at 350°, 12 to 14 minutes. Cool 1 to 2 minutes. Remove to rack. Cool. Divide **Powdered Sugar Frosting** and tint each portion desired color using few drops **food coloring.** Frost cookies. Before frosting sets, pipe on decorative trim with additional icing; decorate with **assorted candies.** For hearts, when frosting is dry, add message.Makes 15.

Christmas Ornaments: On floured surface roll **Basic Dough** to ⅛-inch thickness. Cut into desired shapes with cookie cutters. Place on ungreased cookie sheet. Cut **paper drinking straws** into 1-inch pieces. Push one piece into top of each ornament (*or* make a hole with a skewer). Bake at 350°, 8 to 10 minutes. Remove straw pieces. Cool 1 minute; remove to rack. Cool. Frost one side of ornament with **Royal Frosting.** Add contrasting frosting trim and **decorative candies.** Dry well, about 1½ hours. (For strength frost second side of ornaments. Dry.) Use **colored yarn** for hangers. Makes 72.

Powdered Sugar Frosting: Add enough **milk** to 2 cups sifted **powdered sugar** for easy spreading. Add ¼ teaspoon **vanilla.**

Royal Frosting: Combine 3 **egg whites** (at room temperature), 4½ cups sifted **powdered sugar,** 1 teaspoon **vanilla,** and ½ teaspoon **cream of tartar.** Beat with electric mixer till very stiff, 7 to 10 minutes. Divide into portions and tint each desired color using few drops desired **food coloring.** Keep frosting covered with damp cloth to prevent a crust from forming. (If frosting is too stiff, add water. If too soft, add more sugar.)

Sugar-Molded Decorations

Choose any of the decorations shown on pages 72-73—

With hands mix 3 cups granulated **sugar** and 1 **egg white** thoroughly. Divide sugar mixture into portions. Tint desired color with **food coloring.** Blend with spoon till color is even. Squeeze mixture. When it holds fingerprints, it is moist enough. If too dry, add a few drops **water.** Add more sugar if mixture is too moist.

Cut pieces of **cardboard** large enough to cover molds. Pack sugar firmly to top of desired shape of plastic mold (see picture 1). With spatula, level and scrape excess sugar from top of each mold. Place a piece of cardboard atop sugar. Invert and place on drying surface (see picture 2). Tap mold gently; lift off. Let sugar harden till crust forms (½ hour for small molds; longer for large molds). Hold molded sugar gently in palm of hand (avoid squeezing). Leaving about ¼-inch thick wall, carefully scrape sugar from inside of molds (see picture 3). Dry well.

Easter Egg Baskets: Pipe edge of finished egg half with **Royal Frosting,** if desired. Dry. Fill with **assorted candy** and **decorations.**

Single-Color Bells: Pipe edge and clapper for finished bell with **Royal Frosting.**

Two-Color Bells: Fill mold with one color sugar to ¼ inch from rim. Pack rest of mold with contrasting color sugar. Proceed as above.

Round Ornaments: Prepare two round sugar mold halves as above. Insert **ribbon** or **yarn hanger** between halves. Glue edges of two halves together with **Royal Frosting.** Dry slightly. Pipe on decorative edge.

Diorama Decorations: In two-piece plastic molds, mold two half-sugar eggs *or* balls as above. Immediately after unmolding, use thread to cut a ¾-inch piece from pointed end of each egg half *or* from one side of each ball half. Be sure to hold thread taut. (Do not move either portion of egg or ball half.) Let dry and scoop out as above, discarding ¾-inch pieces. Be sure to form a semicircular well (for half of the peek hole) at cut end of each sugar mold.

Decorate the inside of one of the halves with **Royal Frosting** and desired **plastic figures.** Glue the two halves together with additional frosting. Dry slightly. Pipe a decorative border around seam and edge of peek hole.

Picture 1: Firmly pack wet sugar mixture into plastic molds with spoon. With spatula scrape off excess sugar from mold, making sure sugar is level.

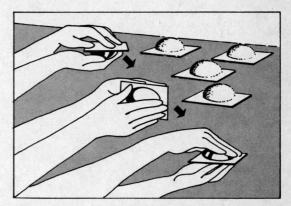

Picture 2: Cut pieces of cardboard large enough to cover mold. Place a piece of cardboard atop packed sugar in mold. Invert and remove plastic mold.

Picture 3: After a crust has formed on sugar molds, gently hold molds in palm of hand (avoid squeezing) and carefully scrape sugar from inside.

How to Give Gifts

Once you've made your food gifts, it would be a shame to have them ruined on the way to their destination. Keeping foods attractive and safe is simple if you follow the hints in this section.

Here you'll learn how to store and pack gifts so they retain their great taste and good looks. You'll also find tips for canning pickles and techniques for sealing jellies and jams.

For special gifts, use the ideas for dressing up foods and combining them with gift containers. Finally discover the chart that shows storage methods and times for the recipes in this book.

Find the right gift for everyone on your gift list from this assortment which includes (clockwise from left) *Cheddar in Red Wine, Sherry-Cheese Spread, Kringla* (in red box), *Stained Glass Fruitcakes* in three shapes, sherry and strawberry variations of *Wine Jelly, Cranberry Cordial, Spiced Lemon Vinegar, Diagonals,* and *Raspberry-Cherry Baskets.* (See Index for page numbers.)

Creative Food Gifts

Half the fun of giving foods gifts is thinking of new ways to give them to friends or relatives for special occasions.

When you need eye-catching gifts, team foods with distinctive containers. Give your homemade liqueur in an elegant decanter, a quick or yeast bread on a wooden bread board, a beverage mix with a mug tree, a cake with a silver cake server, or a cookie jar full of cookies.

For less formal occasions, add sparkle to food gifts by giving them in decorated containers. Turn a shoe box into a train, fire engine, circus wagon, or castle and fill it with candies for a delightful child's gift. Or decorate a rectangular box as a picture frame with your snapshot or a picture of your family in the center and fill it with cookies. This gift will spoil any grandparent or relative living out of town. And fill a new plastic bucket or waste basket with homemade breads, pickles, jellies, or pancake mix and add a big bow for a housewarming gift.

For spur-of-the-moment gifts, make plain foods look special by keeping a few decorating ideas in mind. Decorate plain purchased cookies or homemade cutout cookies with ready-to-use commercial decorator icing in a tube. This gives a quick gift that looks like you've spent hours

making it. Or whip up sandwich cookies by gluing two refrigerator cookies together with a layer of chocolate frosting or your favorite jelly or jam. To dress up a coffee cake, bread, or chiffon cake, dust it with powdered sugar through a paper doily. The design of the doily on your cake or bread will give a professional touch. For a speedy but gracious gift, decorate sugar cubes with a small bow using Royal Frosting and a decorating tube and tip (see recipe, page 84) or commercial decorator's icing. This inexpensive present can be used to add a luxurious note to a buffet or tea table or simply perk up that first cup of coffee in the morning.

Sealing Jellies and Jams

The key to attractive jams and jellies is choosing the right types of jars or glasses and making sure you have them properly sealed.

Start by selecting sturdy jars or glasses which will not break when sterilized and which will withstand the superhot temperatures of jams and jellies. Now decide on the best method of sealing your jars or glasses. There are two suitable sealing materials—standard canning lids with metal screw bands and paraffin. The flat lids and screw bands can be used only on stan-

For an easy fix-up, decorate plain purchased or homemade cookies with commercial icing that comes ready for you to use in a tube.

Using a cake decorating tube and tip and *Royal Frosting* (see recipe, page 84), pipe festive bows on plain sugar cubes to create elegant party favors.

dard canning jars, but paraffin will work with most any type of jelly glass.

To seal jars with metal lids and screw bands: Prepare lids according to manufacturer's directions. Using a wide-mouth funnel, pour the hot fruit mixture into sterilized jars to within ½ inch of top. Working quickly, wipe jar rims, place the metal lids on the jars, and tighten the screw bands. Grasping the jars, one at a time with a pot holder, invert the jars so the hot mixture is against the lids for a few seconds. Then turn the jars upright. Allow them to cool on a rack out of drafts. When the jars are cool, check the seal on each jar by pressing the lid with your fingertip. If the indentation holds after you lift your finger, the jars are sealed.

To seal glasses with paraffin: Melt blocks of paraffin over hot water in an old double boiler. Using a wide-mouth funnel, pour the hot fruit mixture into sterilized glasses to within ½ inch of top. Spoon a thin layer of melted paraffin over the surface of the jelly or jam to seal out air. (Make sure the layer is about $1/16$ inch thick. Too thick a layer of paraffin will cause the jelly or jam to leak around the edges of the paraffin.) Hold the hot glasses, one at a time, with a pot holder and rotate them slowly so the paraffin will cling to the sides of the glasses. Prick any air bubbles. After the paraffin has hardened, spoon another layer of melted paraffin atop so the total depth of both layers is ⅛ inch. Repeat the rotating process.

Pickle and Relish Tips

To insure the best pickles and relishes possible for gift-giving, follow these pickling hints.

Select fresh, firm fruits and vegetables. Fruits are best when slightly underripe. Use pickling salt. Iodized table salt will cause pickles to darken. Use cider vinegar for most pickles. White vinegar can be substituted in light-colored pickles. Unless otherwise directed in a recipe, use granulated white sugar for pickles and relishes. Brown sugar causes color and flavor changes.

Pack pickles or relishes into prepared jars according to recipe directions. Use a flexible spatula to work out air bubbles. Be careful not to cut any pickles. Wipe jar rims adjusting lids and screw bands. Process pickles in boiling water bath according to recipe directions.

After your jars have cooled, check the seal on each jar by pressing the lid with your finger. If the indentation holds after you lift your finger, the jars are sealed. Remove the screw bands, wipe the jars, and label each jar. Store jars in a cool, dark place.

Jellies or jams packed in glasses (at left) should be sealed with paraffin while metal lids and screw bands should be used on canning jars (at right).

Check the seal on a jar of pickles by pressing the lid with your finger. If the indentation holds after you remove your finger, the jar is sealed.

Keeping Baked Goods Fresh

Keep baked food gifts fresh and appealing by storing them properly.

Wrap yeast and quick breads in foil, clear plastic wrap, or in plastic bags and store them in a cool, dry place. (Avoid refrigerating yeast breads since they will become stale more quickly.) To keep breads more than a few days, wrap the unfrosted breads in moisture-vapor-proof freezer wrap and freeze.

For pies, refrigerate those with fillings containing eggs, dairy products, or gelatin. Store fruit pies at room temperature for short periods of time.

When storing cookies, separate crisp and soft varieties—otherwise both will become limp. Store most cookies in containers with tight-fitting lids. Store soft cookies and those with very moist fillings in loosely covered containers. For longer storage freeze baked cookies in freezer containers or foil up to twelve months.

Keep cakes moist by storing them in plastic cake carriers or by covering them with a large bowl. Refrigerate cheesecakes and cakes with cream fillings or frostings that contain egg white. Wrap fruitcakes in moistened cheesecloth and overwrap with foil or clear plastic wrap. If the moistening agent is a nonalcoholic one such as fruit juice, refrigerate fruitcakes.

Store most cookies in containers with tight-fitting lids (foreground). To freeze baked cookies, store in freezer containers (background) or foil.

Packing Pointers

Whether you're packing a cake to carry across town or cookies to mail across the country, there are a few packing tips you should know.

First select foods that travel well. If you are hand-carrying your gift a short distance, almost any food will work, but avoid delicate cakes and pies or foods that spoil easily. If you are mailing a gift, avoid foods in glass containers, yeast breads which become stale quickly, items which must be refrigerated or frozen, and heavily frosted baked goods.

Choose a sturdy container for carrying a gift by hand. A durable dish, cardboard box, or plastic container will do. For mailing, pick a plastic, cardboard, or metal inner container and a heavy cardboard outer box.

Seal your gift in plastic wrap, foil, or in a plastic bag. Then line the container for your gift with plastic wrap, waxed paper, or foil. Place your gift inside the container so it fits securely and will not shift. Fill the spaces with crumpled foil or plastic wrap. Add a layer of foil or wrap on top. Seal the container and decorate, if desired. If the package is to be shipped, label it with the name and address of the person to receive it and place it in a sturdy outer box, making sure it is padded on all sides. Seal and label the box for mailing.

To pack a cake, line a sturdy box with foil. Wrap the cake in clear plastic wrap. Place it in the box and cushion it with plastic wrap or foil.

Gift-Givers Storage Guide

Use this handy chart to help you find the right food gift for your specific needs. Here you will find all the categories of gifts in this book and where the individual recipes can be located. This guide will tell you, at a glance, how far ahead each type of gift can be made, whether it is recommended for mailing, and what its special storage requirements are.

Type of Gift	Page No.	Length of Storage Before Giving	Good Mailers	Storage Directions
Baker's Clay Crafts	82-83	6 to 12 months	No	Keep in a cool place.
Breads, quick	13-15 76-77	2 weeks	Yes	Seal in clear plastic wrap. Keep in a cool place.
Breads, yeast	8-14 77	2-3 days	No	Seal in clear plastic wrap. Keep in a cool place.
Butters	61	2-5 days	No	Refrigerate, covered.
Cakes, Cupcakes	24-29 77	24 hours	No	Cover; keep in a cool place. Refrigerate cakes with cream fillings and frostings made with egg white.
Candy, Brittles, Divinity, Pralines	56-57	2 weeks	No	Cover; keep in a cool place.
Candy, Lollipops and Molds	60	1 month	No	Wrap in clear plastic wrap. Keep in a cool place.
Candy, other	54-60 75, 84	2 weeks	Yes	Cover; keep in a cool place.
Candy Tree	60	6 months	No	Keep in a cool place.
Card and Ornament Cookies	84	2 weeks	Yes	Wrap in clear plastic wrap. Keep in a cool place.
Casseroles	79-81	10 to 12 hours	No	Refrigerate, covered.
Cheesecakes	27	24 hours	No	Refrigerate, covered.
Cookies	16-23 74-75	2 weeks	Yes	Cover; keep in a cool place. Do not mail fragile cookies or those with very moist fillings.
Cordials	71	6 to 12 months	No	Cover; keep in a cool, dark place.
Doughnuts	77	24 hours	No	Cover; keep in a cool place.
Fruitcakes	29	6 weeks	Yes	Wrap in moistened cheesecloth. Overwrap in foil. Keep in a cool place.
Fruits, frozen	34	6 to 8 months	No	Store in freezer.

(continued on next page)

Gift-Givers Storage Guide

Type of Gift	Page No.	Length of Storage Before Giving	Good Mailers	Storage Directions
Fruits, refrigerated	34	1 week	No	Refrigerate, covered.
Fruits, Vegetables, Juices, canned	34-35, 38	6 to 12 months	No	Keep in a cool, dark place.
Jellies, Jams	45-51	6 to 12 months	No	Keep in a cool, dark place.
Jellies, Jams, freezer-type	45, 49, 51	6 to 12 months	No	Store in freezer.
Marzipan Wreath	83	6 months	No	Store in a cool place.
Mixes	64, 69	6 months	Yes	Keep in airtight container.
Mustard	63	2 months	No	Refrigerate, covered.
Pickles, Relishes	39-44	6 to 12 months	No	Keep in a cool, dark place.
Pies	30-31	24 hours	No	Refrigerate, covered.
Popcorn Balls	60	2 weeks	Yes	Wrap in clear plastic wrap. Keep in cool place.
Pretzels	66	2 to 3 days	No	Cover; keep in a cool place.
Salads	78-79	24 hours	No	Refrigerate, covered.
Sauces, canned	61-63	6 to 12 months	No	Keep in cool, dark place.
Sauces, fresh	62-63	1 week	No	Refrigerate, covered.
Sauces, frozen	63	2 months	No	Store in freezer.
Seasonings, dry	64	6 months	Yes	Store in airtight containers.
Snacks, dry	64-67	2 weeks	Yes	Store in airtight container.
Soups	35-36	1 week	No	Refrigerate, covered.
Soups, frozen	36	2 to 4 months	No	Store in freezer.
Spreads, Dips, Cheese Balls	67-68	2 to 3 days	No	Refrigerate, covered or wrapped in clear plastic wrap.
Steamed Puddings	28	24 hours	No	Refrigerate, covered.
Sugar Decorations	85	6 months	No	Keep in cool place.
Vegetables	79-80	10 to 12 hours	No	Refrigerate, covered.
Vinegars	63	2 months	No	Cover; keep in a cool place.

INDEX